MW00467361

True Tales

The Forgotten History of
Michigan's Upper Peninsula

Mikel B. Classen

Modern History Press

Ann Arbor, MI

True Tales: The Forgotten History of Michigan's Upper Peninsula
Copyright © 2022 by Mikel B. Classen. All Rights Reserved

ISBN 978-1-61599-635-3 paperback
ISBN 978-1-61599-636-0 hardcover
ISBN 978-1-61599-637-7 eBook

Published by
Modern History Press   www.ModernHistoryPress.com
5145 Pontiac Trail   info@ModernHistoryPress.com
Ann Arbor, MI 48105

Tollfree 888-761-6268 (USA/CAN/PR) * FAX 734-663-6861

Distributed by Ingram (USA/CAN), Bertram's Books (UK/EU)
Audiobook editions from Audible.com and iTunes

Cover: Reimund Holzey after his arrest in Republic, MI. Standing next to him is Sheriff Glode on the right and his Deputy

Library of Congress Cataloging-in-Publication Data

Names: Classen, Mikel Bruce, 1954- author.
Title: True tales : the forgotten history of Michigan's Upper Peninsula /
  Mikel Bruce Classen.
Description: Ann Arbor, MI : Modern History Press, 2022. | Includes
  bibliographical references and index. | Summary: "A broad survey of
  lesser known but important historical figures, events, and locales in
  Michigan's Upper Peninsula spanning the 18th through 20th centuries.
  Vignettes including such diverse personages as Peter White, Dan Seavey,
  Reimund Holzhey, Mother Ontonagon, and others"-- Provided by publisher.

Identifiers: LCCN 2022001035 (print) | LCCN 2022001036 (ebook) | ISBN
  9781615996353 (paperback) | ISBN 9781615996360 (hardcover) | ISBN
  9781615996377 (epub)
Subjects: LCSH: Upper Peninsula (Mich.)--History. | Upper Peninsula
  (Mich.)--Biography.
Classification: LCC F572.N8 C53 2022 (print) | LCC F572.N8 (ebook) |
DDC
  977.4/9--dc23/eng/20220126
LC record available at https://lccn.loc.gov/2022001035
LC ebook record available at https://lccn.loc.gov/2022001036

Contents

Table of Figures

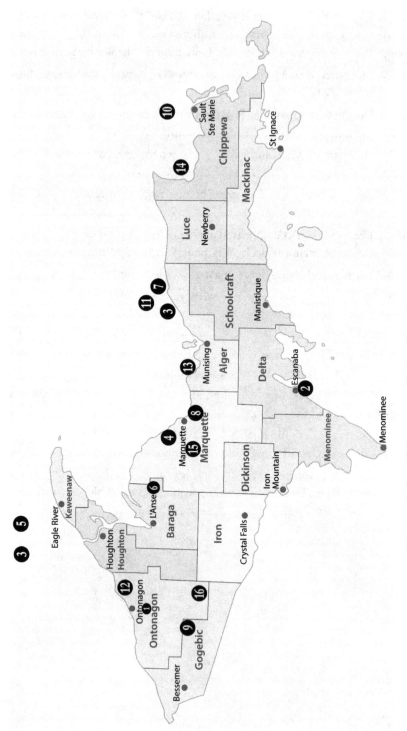

Fig. A-1: Index of chapters in this book on the U.P. Map

Introduction

I've dedicated most of my professional life as a writer to the promotion of the history of Michigan's Upper Peninsula. I've always felt that it was underestimated, under-researched and under-published, and as intriguing as any in the western United States. Because of the combination of mining, maritime and lumbering history, there was a culture created in the U.P. that is unique to the region. It is that uniqueness, mostly overlooked to the present day, that I've worked to bring to light so others can not only learn, but enjoy the tales of the rough and dangerous times of the Upper Peninsula frontier.

Many historians in the past have tried to "romanticize" the history of the U.P. It is a disservice as it lends an inaccurate representation of the true history that created this region. Over the years, those things glossed over are destined to become lost and forgotten forever, lending an almost fantasy illusion of the past.

In this book, the romance is gone. It tries to show many of the true hardships and facets of trying to settle a frontier that was sandwiched between three Great Lakes. There are stories from across the Peninsula from firsthand accounts to revelations from the news of the time. As always there are heroes and villains. There are feats of great good and dirty deeds of the worst kind. There are adventures of the most extraordinary men struggling for the riches of the U.P. well before gold was discovered in California. There are accomplishments of those who braved the wrath of the Great Lakes in leaking ships and frozen waters. The intensity of storms killed thousands on land and lakes. Over 200 died in one season just between Marquette and Whitefish Point. Often the *Edmund Fitzgerald* is memorialized, but few remember the hundreds of wrecks before it. You will find some here.

These pages are populated by Native Americans, and miners, loggers and mariners that consisted of Germans, Italians, Finns, Swedes, French and English. People came from everywhere looking for their personal promised land. Some came to raise families, some to avoid the law or to start a new life, some to get rich no matter what it took. The Upper Peninsula called to all.

The frontier wilderness was deadly, and many humans were dangerous. With the good, came the bad. In the early days, there was no law, and the ones that wore a badge were often on the take or heads of the local criminal elements. Most of the towns were filled with saloons and brothels, where life was cheap and the women were cheaper. Some kidnappers and slavers forced their victims into prostitution. There were thieves and murderers, vigilantes and highwaymen. Lawlessness prevailed in most U.P. towns. Civilizing them was bloody.

This book is the first installment in what will be a larger work that chronicles the rare and forgotten stories that make the history of the U.P. what it is. Through research and investigation, I hope to bring back many of the tales that time and historians forgot.

The U.P. of today was created by individuals who rose up to meet challenges that broke lesser folks. Their mental and physical stamina was that of finely honed athletes, accomplishing feats unheard of in the modern world. They hacked homes out of a dense wilderness and raised families with danger at every turn. Many of these feats have gone unsung throughout history, and many come to light through this book.

I hope that these stories not only celebrate the struggles of the individuals who first braved this formidable and raw land, but honestly portrays their efforts to overcome the incredible obstacles that stood in the way of the beloved peninsula we now know. It was once a very different place.

Mikel B. Classen
March 2022

1

Rock of Ages:
The Tale of the Ontonagon Boulder

Fig. 1-1: On his expedition, Henry Schoolcraft made this drawing of the Ontonagon Boulder along the Ontonagon River. This size of the boulder is hugely out of proportion to the size of the men and canoes

Ever since Europeans heard of the giant piece of copper that the Native Americans worshipped as a gift from the Great Spirit, there was a fervor akin to gold fever to acquire it. The level of effort undertaken to remove the boulder only expresses the extreme to which men will go for greed. This is the beginning, the start of the "copper boom."

First, before I get too deep into this subject, The Native Americans of the Ontonagon were well aware of copper and its uses. Prehistoric copper mines abound throughout the north-western Upper Peninsula. The Ojibwa used it for many things including arrowheads, spear points, jewelry, and trade. They have mined it for thousands of years. Many of the major mining operations we think about today were built on top of prehistoric mine locations. Millions of tons of copper were removed from Isle Royale, the Keweenaw Peninsula and the

Ontonagon region long before recorded Europeans set foot on the continent.

The local Ojibwa believed that the rock had been sent to them by the morning star. It was very powerful in their eyes and was said to speak to them when they blew smoke from a calumet (ceremonial pipe) over the copper. The Natives believed that a voice "full of thunder" would speak to them and demand a human sacrifice. They would normally pick a prisoner of war and burn him at the base of the giant boulder. Sometimes, if the need was great, they would pick a woman.

The earliest written account of the boulder was made by Father Pierre Francois de Charlevoix on his expedition in 1721. He claimed to have witnessed one of these sacrifices:

> "After having a lodge appointed for her use, attendants to meet her every wish, and her neck, arms, and ankles covered with bracelets of silver and copper, she was led to believe that she was to be the bride of the son of the head chief. The time appointed was the end of winter, and she felt rejoiced as the time rolled on, waiting for the season of her happiness. The day fixed upon for the sacrifice having dawned, she passed through all of the preparatory ceremonies and was dressed in her best attire, being covered with all the ornaments the settlement could command, after which she was placed in the midst of a circle of warriors, dressed in their war suits, who seemed to escort her for the purpose of showing their deference. Besides their usual arms, each one carried several pieces of wood, which he had received from the girl. She had carried wood to the rock on the preceding day which she had helped to gather in the forest. Believing that she was to be elevated to a high rank, her ideas being of the most pleasing character, the poor girl advanced to the altar with rapturous feelings of joy and timidity, which would be naturally raised in the bosom of a young female her age. As the procession proceeded, which occupied some time, savage music accompanied them, and chants, invoking that the Great Spirit would prosper their enterprise. Being excited by the music and dancing, the deceitful delusion under which she had been kept remained until the last moment.
>
> "But as soon as they had reached the place of sacrifice, where nothing was to be seen but fires, torches and instruments of torture, her eyes were opened, her fate was revealed to her,

and she became aware of her terrible destiny, as she had often heard of the mysterious sacrifices of the copper rock. Her cries resounded through the forest, but neither tears nor entreaties prevailed. She conjured the stern warriors who surrounded her to have pity on her youth and innocence, but all in vain, as the Indian priests coolly proceeded with the horrid ceremonies. Nothing could prevail against their superstition and the horrid demands of the copper monster, which called for a human sacrifice. She was tied with withes (willow branch) to the top of the rock. The fire was gradually applied to her with torches made of wood she had with her own hands distributed to the warriors. When exhausted with her cries and about expiring, her tormentors opened the circle that had surrounded her, and the great chief shot an arrow into her heart, which was followed by the spears and arrows of his followers, and the blood poured down the sides of the glistening rock in streams. Their weapons were sprinkled with her blood to make them invincible, and all retired to their cabins, cheered and encouraged with the hope of a glorious victory."

Father Charlevoix would go on to explore much of the region, eventually reaching as far south as the mouth of the Mississippi. He kept a journal the entire trip, which is what the preceding was recorded in.

Alexander Henry arrived a few years later, in 1771. He landed at the mouth of the Ontonagon River at the Ojibwa village there. Henry and several other men had been sailing around Lake Superior looking for enough ore of something to make them rich. But stories had found their way to him and he was determined to find the great copper boulder of the Ontonagon River. He was able to hire a couple of Ojibwa men to take him up the river to see the legendary rock. Henry hoped that where there was copper, there might be silver.

Henry estimated that they went 20 miles upriver. His guides pointed out the massive piece of copper. Alexander Henry tells the story:

"I camped at the mouth of the Ontonagon River and took the opportunity of going up the river with Indian guides. The object which I expressly went to see, and to which I had the satisfaction of being led, was a mass of copper, which according to my estimate, weighed no less than five tons. Such was its pure and malleable state that with an axe I was able to cut off a portion weighing one hundred pounds. On viewing the surrounding surface, I conjectured that the mass at some period or other had rolled from the side of a lofty hill which rises at its back."

Henry was so impressed by this that he had his men erect a cabin and they decided to begin mining. This was the first non-native copper mining operation. The men dug, finding some pieces of nice float copper, some weighing more than a pound, but overall, they weren't having much luck. Alexander Henry decided that they would need more supplies and better equipment, so he sailed off to Sault Ste. Marie. His mining operation should be fine until he returned.

When Henry returned, he found his men back at the Ontonagon's mouth waiting for him. Much of the banks of the Ontonagon River is made up of clay. The mine's surrounding clay got wet and the entire operation caved in. It was the end of their venture. They loaded up and went back to Sault Ste. Marie. When Henry published his memoirs a few years later, the legend of the boulder became very well known.

Fifty years later, Henry Rowe Schoolcraft, along with then territorial Governor, Gen. Lewis Cass, saw the boulder on the expedition of Lake Superior in 1819. The expedition was to determine an estimate of the mineral wealth of Lake Superior. At the time the Michigan Territory extended all the way to the Mississippi River. The now rampant rumors of the region's mineral possibilities had piqued Cass' interest. Henry Schoolcraft was appointed as geologist of the expedition and recorded his impressions of the boulder:

> "The rock was found on the edge of a lofty clay bluff, the face of which appears at a former time to have slipped into the river. The shape of the rock is irregular. Its greatest length is three feet, eight inches. Its greatest breadth is three feet, four inches. Altogether it may contain eleven cubic feet. Henry who visited it in 1766 estimated its weight at five tons, but after examining it with scrupulous attention, I do not think the weight of the metallic copper exceeds 2200 pounds. The quantity, however, may have been much diminished since its first discovery, and the marks of chisels and axes upon it, with the broken tools lying around prove that portions have been cut off and carried away."

Fig. 1-2: This is an **exact** replica of the real Ontonagon Boulder. It is identical in shape, size and **weight**. An attempt at chiseling a piece off can be seen in the lower center. The replica sits in the **Ontonagon County Historical Museum** in Ontonagon.

The expedition went on to explore the Lake Superior basin, but the Boulder left a lasting impression on Lewis Cass. A few years later, 1823, Gen. Thomas McKenny and he negotiated a land treaty with the Ojibwa natives. Mineral rights, and specifically the Ontonagon Boulder, were discussed in it. The chief of the Ontonagon tribe, Plover, spoke of the sacred rock like this, "There is a rock there. This, fathers, is the property of no one man. It belongs to all of us. It was put there by the Great Spirit, and it is ours. In the life of my father the British were busy working it. It was then big, like that table. They tried to raise it to the top of the hill but failed. They then said the copper was not in the rock but in the banks of the river. They dug for it by a light, working underground. The earth fell in, killing three men. It was then left until now."

Once the treaty was signed, an immediate attempt was made to recover the boulder and bring it out of the Ontonagon River to the mouth. A company of men was detached to the Ontonagon country to begin immediate recovery of the legendary copper mass. Underestimating what it would take to perform such an operation, the wilderness of Ontonagon would show how formidable it could be. George Porter, one of men on the expedition, describes the journey:

"With two boats and twenty men, including our Indian guide, we proceeded up the river. About twenty-eight miles from its mouth, the river divided into two branches of equal magnitude. We continued up the right branch for about two miles further, where we found it necessary to leave our boats and proceed by land. After travelling about five miles on foot over points of mountains from one to three hundred feet high, all separated by deep ravines, the bottoms of which were bogs and which by thick underbrush were rendered impervious to the rays of the sun, we came to the object of our search, long known as the 'Copper Rock' of Lake Superior. This remarkable specimen of virgin copper lies a little above the low water mark on the west bank of the river about thirty-five miles from its mouth. Having ascertained that with our means and time it was impossible to remove by hand a body weighing more than a ton, we proceeded to examine the channel of the river. We found it to be intercepted by ridges of sandstone, forming cataracts, with a descent in all of about seventy feet over which it was impossible to pass, while high perpendicular banks of sandstone rendered passage around them impracticable. Finding our plans completely frustrated by unforeseen difficulties, we were obliged to abandon our attempt."

In the late 1830s, Douglass Houghton came into the region. He had been named State Geologist for the budding new State of Michigan. No longer a territory, Michigan had been awarded the Upper Peninsula as compensation for a strip of land that included Toledo that was awarded to Ohio in what was known as the Toledo War, also called the Michigan/ Ohio War. Houghton set off on an expedition of his own to specifically assess the mineral wealth that could be found in the U.P. This was the first real geological survey of the Lake Superior region. It set into motion what is now known as the "Copper Boom," one of the

biggest mineral rushes of all time. Houghton addressed the famed boulder in his final mineralogical report in 1841. "I have thus far not alluded particularly to the large mass of native copper which has long been known to exist in the bed of the Ontonagon River. While this mass of native copper cannot fail to excite much interest for its size and purity, it must be borne in mind that it is a perfectly isolated mass having no connection with any other; nor does the character of the country lead to the inference that any veins of the metal occur in the

Fig. 1-3: James K Paul, founder of Ontonagon and the man that wrestled the great copper mass from its resting place along the Ontonagon River.

immediate vicinity, though the mineral district crosses the country at a distance of a few miles."

Two things occurred in 1841-43 that led to one of the greatest mineral rushes in history: Houghton's report and the retrieval of the "Copper Boulder." Though rumored to have existed for many years and having been seen by only a few, the Ontonagon Boulder was finally revealed to the world, removing it from the realm of mythology into fact. It is rare in history when one moment can be pinpointed that changes everything, but the Copper Boom begins with the Ontonagon Boulder.

How it was retrieved is a bit murky. Two men claimed to have pulled it from its resting place along the river. There is no doubt there is some braggadocio involved with the retelling, but through multiple sources some semblance of the story can be pieced together. One thing is sure, both men were involved in pulling the stone free from the Ontonagon River.

The two men are James K. Paul and Julius Eldred. Both claimed to have retrieved the boulder, but one of their stories simply doesn't hold up. The real accomplishment was done by James K. Paul. Born in Virginia, he was a veteran of the Blackhawk war.

He had heard of the boulder from a Nicholas Minclergue, who told him the tale of the boulder that lay on the west branch of the Ontonagon River. In 1842, he decided to go look for and sell the Ontonagon Boulder. With Minclergue, who worked as an interpreter throughout the expedition, the pair mounted an expedition from Wisconsin into the depths of the Ontonagon country. It was a hard-fought expedition, as the pair soon realized that the mules they had purchased wouldn't be able to make the journey. They sold them and then proceeded with canoes down the Wisconsin River, portaged to the Montreal River to Lake Superior. They then followed the coast to the mouth of the Ontonagon River. Here they built a small cabin on the north side of the river. This became his base of operations as well as the beginning of Ontonagon as a village. J.K. Paul was the founder of Ontonagon.

1842 was the year that the Ojibwas signed a treaty with the Federal Government, ceding the region to the U.S., but since it wasn't yet ratified the local Natives were very suspicious of Paul when he and Minclergue began asking questions about the boulder and its location. Most refused to answer him. There is evidence that Julius Eldred, a businessman from Detroit, had traveled there the previous year with Samuel Ashmun from Sault Ste. Marie and purchased the boulder from the Ojibwa. Having made a deal with Eldred, they were unwilling to talk. Eldred had then returned to Detroit, expecting to come back later and extract the boulder.

Proceeding up the river on his own, Paul began a long search for the boulder. Eventually he found it lying on the banks of the river, partly submerged in water. He built a cabin within fifty feet of the boulder, and then cleared the brush in between so he could watch his prize from the cabin.

He made plans to take the boulder out of the wilderness to his other cabin at the mouth of the river. As discovered by those who had previously attempted to acquire the rock, logistics was going to be difficult at best. Between the rock and Lake Superior were several sets of rapids as well as a substantial waterfall that would make floating it downriver impossible for at least the first three miles. He devised another plan. Using a line and capstan seemed to be his only option. Pulling the rock up to the top of a several-hundred-foot-bluff was an accomplishment in itself, but the boulder was pulled nearly three miles through the woods. He then began work on a road to get the nearly two-ton boulder. He built movable tracks and a low cart to haul the boulder on. It was then that the winter of 1842-43 rolled in. He had to stop all work until the next spring. He spent the winter in his "rock" cabin.

As spring came, he renewed his work. He had just finished preparing to begin moving the boulder when he got a surprise. It was the arrival of Major Walter Cunningham and Julius Eldred, accompanied by a group of natives. Eldred was returning to claim his property. Over the winter, the treaty had been ratified and the Secretary of War, John C. Calhoun, had instructed Cunningham to "Secure the rock," which had achieved the status of legend. He was ordered to bring it to Washington.

Paul was having none of it. He pulled a pistol and claimed the rock by preemption, as he had homesteaded the property, so by rights it was his. He was willing to shoot anyone who tried to take it away. After long discussion, the stand-off was ended by coming to the agreement that Paul would move the boulder to the mouth of the Ontonagon River and then receive a reasonable compensation. Paul's original plan had been to sell the boulder, so this was agreeable to him. Cunningham and Eldred withdrew and with the help of some of the natives was able to get the boulder far enough downriver that it was eventually able to be loaded into a large boat to be floated the rest of the way to the mouth and then placed in Paul's cabin.

It wasn't long before Maj. Cunningham returned with Eldred on a revenue cutter. Cunningham entered into negotiations with James Paul, but he wasn't offering enough. Frustrated and angry, Cunningham ordered the Captain of the schooner to load the rock immediately. Again Paul wasn't having any of it. He pulled his gun. He then promised to make a corpse of the first man who touched his boulder until he gave them permission. The crew of the cutter believed him and refused to follow the Major's orders.

Julius Eldred stepped in and paid Paul with a check for $1,800, no small sum in 1843. Eldred was figuring on getting reimbursed from the Federal Government. James Paul went on to find other large pieces of mass copper, all of them larger than the Ontonagon Boulder. It is not true that the Ontonagon Boulder is the largest piece of pure copper found, it is simply the most famous.

The boulder was loaded aboard the revenue cutter, *Algonquin*. Julius Eldred had originally planned to put the boulder on display and take it on tour around the country, but Major Cunningham had been ordered to take possession of the boulder and was told to compensate whoever claimed ownership up to $700. Eldred had spent $1,100 more than that trying to get it out of James Paul's hands without the gunplay that would have surely ensued. Major Cunningham was in the midst of a dilemma. He decided to let Eldred maintain temporary possession of it.

The *Algonquin* sailed to Sault Sainte Marie. This was a decade before there were locks at the Soo, so the boulder had to be portaged around the Sault rapids. Loaded onto a cart, the copper boulder was rolled down what is now Portage Ave. to the docks below the rapids. It was loaded onto a schooner called the Brewster, which then set sail for Detroit.

The news of the Ontonagon copper rock spread like wildfire and by the time the ship arrived in Detroit, it was big news. Eldred,who had always had intentions of touring and displaying the rock, realized that his dream might still be realized. Since Cunningham had given him custody of the rock, he immediately made plans to display it at 25 cents a head. When they docked, with full pomp and circumstance, he had the boulder pulled through town with four black horses on an overly decorated wagon. He had the showmanship of a P.T. Barnum.

Whether he decided this way back in Ontonagon or something that occurred to him in Detroit, Eldred claimed he'd brought the boulder. Piecing together a tale worthy of Barnum that included details of how Paul had accomplished the feat, he developed a story of adventure and daring for his customers viewing the displayed rock. He even claimed at one point that he had leaned over a cliff where the boulder was protruding and by hand cut through six inches of solid copper until it fell to the river below. Eldred told his story so wel, that there is a controversy over J.K. Paul and Julius Eldred as to who really brought the boulder out. It was just simpler for Eldred to claim credit so he could dazzle his audience as they paid their admission. Unfortunately, the inconsistency in his story makes it easier to discount him as the actual discoverer. Also claiming that he was the one who accomplished the feat would come in handy later on.

It is unclear as to how long Eldred was actually allowed to display the boulder, but it was not long after that the government stepped back in and reclaimed the copper mass. This time they wouldn't be deterred. The Ontonagon boulder was loaded onto another schooner and shipped off to Buffalo, NY. Again, as it was moved from the ship, Eldred made sure that the great Copper Rock received its due attention. As the boulder was on its way to the railroad yard, it was paraded through Buffalo. Again, a huge crowd turned out and it is said that many tried to chip pieces off it as it moved through the streets. Again it was decorated aboard a four-wheel horse-drawn truck.

Eldred had been promised by Cunningham that he would be able to receive the copper rock when it arrived at Georgetown. He did, and oversaw the Ontonagon Boulder being placed in the yard of the United States War Department. It was the end of an era for Eldred.

He spent the next two years attempting to get reimbursed for his expenses from Congress. It is here that his story of pulling the boulder through the wilderness was beneficial. It certainly would have bolstered his claims of expenses far beyond the original $700. Eventually the government paid him $5,664.98. The *Congressional Record* states that he was paid for "his time and expense in purchasing and removing the mass of copper commonly called 'the copper rock'."

It stayed in the yard at the War Department until the Civil War, then was moved to a corner of the National Museum. It makes sense that a large amount of copper during the civil war would have been quite a prize for the Confederacy. In its place at the national Museum, the boulder was forgotten.

In 1902, an Ontonagon newspaper editor, Alfred Meads, found it collecting dust in a corner and completely unidentified. Mead tells the story in his own words:

> "In the winter of 1880-81, I was in Washington and wanted to see the rock. Jay A. Hubbell was then our member of congress. He had never seen it and requested me to hunt it up. Two days' search in the Navy Yard failed to locate it.

"I afterward found it in the Smithsonian Institute. No one knew of its whereabouts. Finally one of the workmen in the basement said there was a big piece of copper rock in the packing room and we found it stowed away in a dark, out of the way corner. It was described as a copper rock found on the Ontonagon and supposed to have been used as an altar by the Indians. Mr. Hubbell and myself secured the promise of the officers in charge of the museum that it should be placed on a pedestal in the museum proper and labeled 'Copper Rock found and taken out of the Ontonagon River, in the Upper Peninsula of Michigan, by James K. Paul of Ontonagon.' Since that time, I have never seen it."

Over the years there have been stories of the Smithsonian losing track of the 3,708 pound rock; not an easy feat but the government seems adept at it. Over the years Ontonagon residents have tried to get the boulder returned to what is considered its rightful home. The Smithsonian's seeming disinterest in the rock has prompted calls for its return. But as interest rises, the Smithsonian's grip on the artifact has tightened with each inquiry.

There was an exact replica made, which was originally displayed at Michigan Tech University in Houghton. The replica now resides in the Ontonagon County Historical Society Museum. It is exact in every way, including visible chisel marks.

The Ontonagon Boulder was not the biggest piece of mass copper ever found. The mining days unearthed masses of copper that make the boulder look like a pebble. But its legend and fame alone brought about the copper boom. Without the stories it spawned, there might never have been a Copper Country.

2   Captain Dan Seavey
Escanaba Buccaneer

Fig. 2-1: Captain Dan Seavey the notorious pirate that sailed the Great Lakes.

It took many unusual individuals to create the unique, rich history of the Upper Peninsula, so it should not be surprising that among them was a pirate. Back in its infancy, the Upper Peninsula was considered a territory of limitless prospect with its rich mineral and timber resources. Another of its resources was the vast Great Lakes that also provided opportunities, not only for shipping and fishing, but also for marauding. In the late 1800s, law enforcement on the water was practically nonexistent. The lakes were the location of all kinds of smuggling, poaching, even piracy. Dan Seavey, a schooner captain who docked in Escanaba, was a pirate who sailed out into the lakes and plundered wherever and whatever he could.

Born in Portland, Maine in 1865, Dan Seavey grew up around sailing and had the love of the sea in his heart. He spent all of his free time around the ships and the men who sailed them. Enchanted with the idea of the sea, he ran away from home at the age of thirteen to sail on tramp steamers. As soon as he was old enough he joined the Navy. He wasn't one to take orders well, and when his hitch was up, he honorably departed.

Fig. 2-2: Dan Seavey's ship the *Wanderer*. Sometimes it acted as a floating brothel.

Next, he tried working at catching smugglers and trespassers for the Bureau of Indian Affairs on Indian reservations in Wisconsin and Oklahoma. Still dissatisfied, he moved to Milwaukee where he set himself up in the commercial fishing business and opened a fish market. His love for the sea was reawakened and a love for the Great Lakes was born.

He got married, bought a farm and fathered a daughter. However, a few years down the road, he caught gold fever and left everything to move to Alaska during the gold rush. He returned from the goldfields empty-handed and broke.

Upon his return in the early 1890s, he settled in Escanaba where he opened a small freight boat service. Seavey acquired a schooner named the Wanderer, where he lived part of the time. He also had a room in a boarding house in downtown Escanaba and, in later years, bought a permanent home.

He sailed out of the harbor with a small crew, the first to leave in the spring and the last to arrive in the winter, arriving back as the harbor was closing with ice, rigging and spars covered with icicles, the deck caked with snow, battered from braving the early winter storms.

Most of the local sailors considered him slightly crazy, a notion later confirmed in their eyes.

Using his freight service as a cover, Seavey entered a port after dark with no lights on, then he and his crew loaded everything on board that could be found and set sail before daybreak. He looted anything he could get: cattle, hay, leather goods, and fruit—even women. All that was accessible on the docks that could be loaded before dawn would be gone. Upon the boat's return to Escanaba, he sold it all as legitimate cargo and reap the profits.

Seavey loved children and spent time talking with them whenever he could. The boys of Escanaba faithfully waited at the docks for his return. He told them stories for hours on end and taught a couple of the boys to sail. One Escanaba boy had been sitting and talking to Seavey for most of the day about sailing and a sailor's life, enthralled with the romance of it. Upon leaving the ship, the boy's father grabbed him and spanked him right there on the docks. As he turned to escort his son home, a hand gripped his shoulder and spun him around. The father found himself staring into Dan Seavey's huge chest. Seavey took the father (a prominent businessman) down and resoundingly spanked him, telling him to "leave my shipmates alone."

Dan unloaded some of his plundered and illegal goods in Chicago. It was an entry into the black market where no questions were asked. Shipment was always accepted regardless of the type of cargo and payment was immediately made in cash. Seavey refused to become the agent of any one faction of the underworld, selling to whoever came up with the cash first. This flaunting of independence made him many enemies on both sides of the law.

Seavey had many hideouts throughout Lake Michigan, and had a homestead on St. Marin's Isle. From there he ran contraband venison to Chicago in the fall when meat was scarce. The Booth Fish Company, a Chicago-based market with ties to the underworld, wanted Seavey's venison empire. They sent a gang out on one of their boats to take over his territory. After a vicious fight, he was chased away by overwhelming odds. Victorious, the gang started back to Chicago with their news of success. It was just about dusk when Seavey caught up with them in the *Wanderer*. Again a tough fight ensued, but this time the pirate had equalized the odds by bringing a cannon that he had pilfered, and mounted it on the bow of the boat. The fight ended when Seavey blew the other boat out of the water. None of the gang ever returned to

Chicago and Seavey made it well known that the same fate was in store for anyone else who tried to cross him.

Dan Seavey loved to fight. He had a standing challenge that he would always go a few rounds with anyone who thought they could take him. He once sailed to Manistee just to fight a man who had a reputation for having never been beaten. Another incident occurred in Frankfort, where Dan fought a man named Mike Love, in a large circle drawn on the ice in the bay. The fight was much publicized and there was a large turnout from the residents. Betting on the outcome seemed to be the spectators' main concern while the two men battled in the snow and cold. It was reported that blows were exchanged for nearly two hours before Dan Seavey finally emerged victorious and announced that drinks would be on him at the nearest saloon.

Seavey salvaged wrecks and lured some ships to their doom by putting out false buoys, running them aground. After a wreck, Seavey would wait out of sight on the *Wanderer* until the crew abandoned ship. Then he transferred their cargo to his ship, sail off, and sell it. This buoy trick had other uses, too.

Seavey once got the crew of the *Nellie Johnson* drunk in Charlevoix, overpowered her captain, tied him up in chains and tossed him over the side. He then took the schooner to Chicago and sold the ship and the cargo. When he returned to Frankfort, a wealthy man hired him to sail a yacht to Mackinac. Seavey didn't know it at the time, but the man had set him up. As Seavey sailed past Port Betsie, a revenue cutter named the *Tuscarora* slipped out of the darkness and took up pursuit. It had waited out of sight in a cove until Seavey passed it. The chase went on throughout much of the night but Seavey knew the waters much better than the crew of the cutter. As he passed a harbor buoy, Seavey shot the light out and replaced it with a lantern on a barrel. The *Tuscarora* ran aground, but a change in the wind direction also changed Seavey's luck. The stranded cutter fired a cannon shot across the yacht's bow and he was forced to surrender.

He was taken to Chicago in chains to stand trial for pirating the *Nellie Johnson*. When he appeared before the judge, he cleverly explained that the captain of the schooner was drunk and had given him the ship and cargo in settlement of an old debt. Because the former captain of the *Nellie Johnson* couldn't be found to dispute Seavey's claim, the case fell apart and Dan was released. Ironically, he was then deputized as a U.S. Marshall. The Great Lakes had been nearly impossible to patrol and the law difficult to enforce. It was decided that instead of chasing Seavey, they would get him to take the job of patrolling the waters and enforcing the law. The illegal whiskey smuggling, unlawful fishing, contraband venison and rampant theft had to be stopped, and Seavey could get into places where regular lawmen couldn't. Also, with Dan now on the side of the law, a good portion of the illegal activities were expected to cease because he was a major contributor. Seavey saw it as his chance to start over again, but just because he was now a lawman, his wild ways didn't really change.

He tracked down an outlaw who had been stealing and selling whiskey to the Indians. Dan located him in a saloon in Naubinway. The outlaw told him, "If you can drag me outside, I'll board your schooner for Chicago." After a few drinks the fight started. Literally, hours of fighting followed, wrecking the saloon. The two occasionally stopped for a drink or two of whiskey. Finally Seavey slammed the outlaw against the bar, breaking most of the bottles of liquor. Afraid that there wouldn't be enough whiskey left to finish the fight, he knocked the man down and placed a piano on his neck. After downing a few more shots of whiskey, he reconsidered and lifted the piano off the outlaw and asked him to join him in a drink before resuming the fight. The outlaw never got up. He died the following day. Marshall Seavey turned the body over to officials to be buried, and turned in his report. He was never asked to answer for the killing.

While Seavey had a long lucrative career, making well over a million dollars in his lifetime in illegal activities, he wasn't as hard-hearted as his occupation made him seem. He gave away all of his money to the poor and to benefit children.

When Seavey died in an old folk's home in Peshtigo, Wisconsin in 1949, he died quietly, penniless: an end quite unbefitting the wild and rowdy buccaneer who often said he would rather fight than eat.

3   The Lightkeeper Hero and the Wrecks of the *Monarch* and *Kiowa*

Fig. 3-1: SS Monarch underway (courtesy Wikipedia)

In the early days of settling the Lake Superior frontier, life was a constant battle with danger, and a life-and-death situation could arise in the flash of a moment. This was particularly true when sailing the moody water of Lake Superior. Late season travel was the most dangerous of all. From October through November, shipwrecks were common, loss of life not unusual. It is during these situations that heroes show themselves.

In December of 1906, a passenger steamer named the *Monarch* left Port Arthur, Canada during the beginning of a blinding snowstorm. The ship carried forty-one passengers bound for Sarnia, Ontario, which was on the southern tip of Lake Huron. The snow was thick and blinding. Visibility was only a few feet. The Captain of the ship,

Edward Robertson, a thirty-five-year veteran of the lakes, had been sailing on a compass heading as the surf began to build and the winds turned to a gale. Unsure of his position, the Captain ordered a check on what was known as the "log," a cylinder that trailed behind the ship recording mileage.

Visibility was near zero, but a break in the blizzard showed a light in the distance. The mate on watch reported to the Captain that he had spotted the Passage Island Light. That simply couldn't be. In the Captain's estimation, there was no conceivable way that they had traveled that far. It was simply too soon. What was the light then?

The *Monarch* kept churning its way through the darkness and blinding snow. The propellers were working hard. The Captain had hoped to outrun the storm front, or at least to break out of the blizzard. The Monarch was sailing at full speed when it hit the rocks. Water poured into the stern as seams broke from the impact.

Captain Robertson immediately assessed the desperate situation of his ship. He had to keep it afloat. If she slipped off the rocks, there was a good chance everyone would drown. He ordered the engines to be kept running at all costs. Water was pouring into the engine room, but the boilers were still fired and the crew did their best. With the propeller turning, the force kept the bow against the rocks.

It was now early morning and in the dim light, the Captain and crew could make out Blake's Point on Isle Royale. They now knew their location and they could see the treacherous rock shoreline. The only way off the ship would be to run a line from the ship to the rocks on the shore. One of the crew, Watchman J. Jacques, volunteered to take one of the small lifeboats ashore to string a line. They lowered the boat and the surf was rough. It tossed the boat around, but Jacques valiantly rowed to the rocky shore. The waves rose and slammed the little boat down on the rocks, breaking it into splinters. Watchman Jacques was thrown into the water. Struggling was futile. He was Lake Superior's now.

The crew and passengers watched as their companion drowned. But there was no time to dwell on the loss. Time was running out and they still had to get off. A new plan was formed. Another volunteer was tied to a long rope, lowered to just above the surf and then swung to shore, hopefully close enough to grab onto one of the rocks and pull himself ashore. Different sources give him various names.

Like a giant pendulum he was swung back and forth and when they thought he was close enough, he was released and they missed. He fell

Fig. 3-2: Bow of the *SS Monarch* at the Palisades, winter of 1907 (Isle Royale National Park Archives)

into the surf, only to be pulled back to the ship and out of the water. Again the swinging and again the release. Another miss.

He was hauled up for a third attempt and they started swinging again. Out the rope stretched, and it broke! The momentum carried the man toward the shore, and by his fingertips, he was able to catch onto a rock. He pulled himself up, wet and cold. At least he was on the shore.

The crew on the ship, using a long ladder, ran a new line across and the deckhand had to then climb to the top of the rocky cliff. When he reached the top, he tied the rope to a tree and it was pulled tight. Now the passengers and crew had a way to safety as long as the ship stayed afloat.

The stern had submerged, but the bow clung to the rocks. The crew and passengers now had to go one at a time, hand over hand, above the rolling surf to the rocks on the shore. Each one made the dramatic crossing, including one elderly woman.

One man, a watchman, grabbed the wrong line and went into the water. Quickly, Lake Superior claimed his life.

The rest made it successfully with the Captain waiting to be the last off his ship. The cold, wet group huddled around each other at the top of the rocks. They watched as the bow of the Monarch rose to a fifty-degree angle and the unmanned engines finally quit. The stern broke

Fig. 3-3: Passage Island Lighthouse guarding the primary maritime passage between Thunder Bay and the open lake (NPS / Paul Brown)

and sank into the lake. The bow stayed where it was, the waves battering it mercilessly.

Now there were more pressing matters: staying alive. They began collecting driftwood for a fire. One of the passengers was carrying matches that were still usable. It wasn't long and they had one started. The Captain hoped that the fire would signal any passing ships, though he knew that every day that passed, that hope would get slimmer. Theirs had been the last run of the season for the *Monarch*, few other ships would be passing this late in the year. Their situation was desperate.

A few miles away stood the Passage Island Lighthouse. The head lightkeeper, Mr. Shaw, could see the smoke of the fire from his tower. He called his Assistant Lightkeeper, Klaus Hamringa to help take bearings and to keep a watch on the smoke column to determine if it was stationary or moving. They came to the conclusion that it was stationary and probably a fire of some stranded fishermen.

They decided to keep watch on it. Lake Superior was still rough and the winds were still blowing a gale. The pair decided that when the lake calmed, one of them would go and take a look.

The survivors of the Monarch were actively working to keep themselves alive. They gathered brush and branches and made a makeshift windbreak. Some flour and frozen salmon washed ashore from the wreck and they managed to get it ashore. The little food helped. They were in a dire situation. It was cold enough that a few feet away from the fire, fingers and ears could freeze. Forty-one people huddled around a fire, trying to keep from freezing.

Four of the men knew of a hunting camp at Tobin Harbor, some twelve miles away. The four decided to strike out, hoping to recover some food from the camp and maybe, if they were lucky, someone might be there to help. It was a long, hard trek and when they got there, they found it deserted and by all appearances, it had been for a while. They did find some provisions, but not much. They hiked back to the survivor camp and added the food to the community stores.

After two days, Lake Superior began to calm. The gale winds had abated some. The lightkeepers at Passage Island were still watching the smoke from the fire of the survivors. The pair decided that Lake Superior was calm enough that one of them could go to investigate, thinking that some fishermen had gotten in trouble. It was against the rules of the Lighthouse Service to abandon the lighthouse completely, so only one could go. Assistant Keeper Hamringa was the logical choice.

He readied the lighthouse's rowboat and set out toward the smoke. Lake Superior was still rough, and there was the sharp, icy cold of winter still in the wind. He had packed himself some lunch and had the foresight to take some woolen blankets. He also ensured that he had dry matches along. Hamringa knew in the back of his mind that there was the possibility that he himself could become shipwrecked.

Hamringa had been shipwrecked twice before: once off the banks of Newfoundland and once while rounding the Cape of Good Hope. Now, he was always prepared for the worst and hoped for the best. He continued to row hard against the rolling waves. Snow squalls still passed over obscuring his view and forcing him to keep the shore in sight. It was a four-mile row that took several hours to complete, but finally as he rowed around the rocks of Blake's Point, he saw what was left of the *Monarch*.

The bow was still wedged between the rocks, covered with a layer of snow. Hamringa rowed the boat over where the stern should have been, but the drop was so deep, he could see nothing of it. He rowed toward the shore. There was nowhere he could land due to the steep cliffs, so he kept the boat offshore. He shouted. There was no response, but he knew someone had kept a fire going for several days. He shouted again. There was movement on the rock bluff above.

Fig. 3-4: The tug *James Whalen,* which rescued the *Monarch* (George N. Fletcher Library, Alpena)

The stranded passengers and crew of the *Monarch* weren't expecting help. They were huddled together around a smoky fire. They had constructed a crude shelter out of spruce and balsam branches and were beginning to suffer frostbite. Though the weather had subsided, it didn't help their situation. Then they heard the shouts from lightkeeper Hamringa.

They ran to the top of the ridge yelling and waving handkerchiefs and hats. Hamringa responded, yelling and waving back. He didn't have room to take everyone, but shouted up to them, "Is there one of you who can row a boat? We'll go back to the lighthouse and bring back help!"

The group talked amongst themselves and the purser of the Monarch, Mr. Beaumont, volunteered. There are two differing stories about how the purser got to Hamringa. The first was that Beaumont was lowered down the ice-covered face of the rock by the survivors above. He waited until he was within jumping distance of the rowboat and was able to land inside.

The other version has Beaumont jumping into the water and swimming to the side of the rowboat while Hamringa pulled him in.

However he got there, lightkeeper Hamringa was able to get him wrapped in blankets and they began the long row back to the Passage

Island Light. Beaumont was given the lunch that Hamringa had packed. Several hours later, they made it back.

Mr. Shaw, the head lightkeeper, spotted a steamer named the *Edmonton*, which had just left Port Arthur and was able to signal it with the fog signal. The *Edmonton* hove to and Shaw and Hamringa took Beaumont out to it. The captain listened to Beaumont's tale of the shipwreck and was told how many people were still left out there.

Realizing that a ship of that size wouldn't be able to get anywhere near the wreck site, the captain turned his ship back towards Port Arthur to get help. Shaw and Hamringa went back to their lighthouse. Beaumont went with the Edmonton.

Arriving back in Port Arthur, the captain of the *James Whalen*, a large, stable tugboat, was roused from his bed. He was sick, but when he heard of the predicament of the Monarch survivors, he jumped to the emergency. Loading twenty tons of extra coal, blankets, food, medical supplies, and two doctors, the tug was loaded for rescue.

The sail to Isle Royale was long and rough, but as the day passed, the weather was favorable.

The *James Whalen* was frequently used as an icebreaker. As they pulled into the rocky site of the Monarch wreck, the tossing surf forced the captain to hold the tug offshore. Seeing no one, the *Whalen* sounded its whistle four times.

At the top of the ridge, figures could be seen floundering in the snow above as the passengers and crew of the *Monarch* ran toward the sound of the whistle. As the survivors watched, the tug moved around to the lee side of Blake's Point and lowered its lifeboats, landing a party on the shore. They hiked from there to the survivors who were rapidly making their way to them, slipping through the snow and tumbling over the deadfalls.

They were taken on board and fed hot food and were covered with blankets. The doctors went around treating frostbite in several of the survivors' feet and hands. They had all survived, including the elderly lady passenger. She was complimented as the "best man of the party." Several passengers expressed regret that they hadn't saved their one and only axe that had kept the 41 people alive through the harsh weather. It would have made an interesting souvenir. They had been stranded on Isle Royale for four brutal, long days. If they hadn't been rescued when they were, there would have been much more loss of life and certainly the frostbite would have led to loss of limbs.

Klaus Hamringa, the lightkeeper who rowed to the party, was given a commendation for valor from the Lighthouse Service. His heroism did not go unnoticed. He was again instrumental in saving survivors of another shipwreck several years later when he was transferred to Au Sable Point Lighthouse.

In 1923, Klaus L. Hamringa came to Au Sable Point Lighthouse of Grand Marais, Michigan. It was a rough and lonely place, much like Isle Royale had been. Now, at Au Sable, he was head lightkeeper.

His years there as lightkeeper were relatively uneventful. There were no major wrecks, ships were now being built to take rough seas as routine. Steel ships had been gradually replacing the timber-hulled ones, most of which had sunk or were retired as being slow and inefficient. Any companies that could afford to replace them did, which was cutting down on the losses of both ships and lives. With fewer losses, there were higher profits. Post World War I, steel ship construction was stepped up to an all-time high. Iron was in high demand. Losses during the war had caused a rebuilding of not only the naval power of the United States, but also of the shipping freighters. A frequent target of the war, there had been considerable losses of commercial transport ships. The reconstruction of the shipping fleet was a priority.

The nature of Au Sable Point, a long sandstone reef six feet under the surface, created dangerous moments, but they had been of a smaller scale than previous years. Hamringa writes," Polishing whistles and cleaning in tower, fisherman from Grand Marais, windbound at station. Had to pull his boat up on the boatway. Blowing hard from west." The next day, "Fisherman left for Grand Marais this morning. Had to walk and leaving boat at station and are glad for saving the boat and nets. Blowing Gale."

Hamringa had a bit of a sense of humor as well. The entry for August 27, 1928 shows it. "Working in yard. A porcupine visited station. (didn't invite him back.)"

For Hamringa, all was quiet and routine at Au Sable. That was until his last year, 1929. Ahead was that light at the end of the tunnel called retirement. His years of hard work would be over.

It was a season of storms and it was the time of shipwrecks. In August, a tug named the Barrallton was towing a 313-foot barge named *Lake Frugality*. They were heading toward Au Sable and Sault Ste. Marie when they were hit by a storm from out of the northeast. The tug was heading into the face of it and the waves were building.

Fig. 3-5: *Kiowa,* a package freigher (George N. Fletcher Library, Alpena)

Suddenly, the cable snapped and the *Lake Frugality* was floating free, at the mercy of rising seas. Fortunately, she didn't sink but grounded ashore along the beach west of the lighthouse. The tug proceeded on until it got on the lee side of Whitefish Point. With a northeast blow, it would never have been able to get into Grand Marais harbor for refuge.

The Coast Guard arrived at the stranded ship. Seeing that it wasn't in peril of sinking, the small crew was left aboard. Three days later the Barrallton made it back and with the help of the Coast Guard, they were able to get it free and back under tow.

At the end of August, another storm blew up. The Alice L. was a gasoline fishing tug that was caught in a fast storm just east of Au Sable. Few details are known about the wreck, but when the Alice L. sank, it took someone with it. The icy cold of Superior claimed another soul.

Keeper Hamringas's tenure was almost through. He was going to retire and tell stories to his grandchildren. Little did he know, there were more stories to be made. They would be closing the lighthouse for the season in just a few days. November 29, 1929 saw a storm move in from the north. It rapidly turned into a blizzard.

Steaming toward Au Sable was a freighter named the *Kiowa*, a sister ship to the *Lake Frugality* that had run ashore a couple months earlier.

Her holds were full of flax seed headed for Chicago. The blizzard caught up with the ship, then it engulfed it. The ever-growing seas were rough and they tossed the steamer helplessly. Suddenly, the entire cargo of seed shifted to one side, causing the Kiowa to have a terrible list. It was so bad that water was coming in the portholes.

Captain Alex T. Young was terrified and ordered nine of his men into one of the lifeboats. He then got in himself and ordered the lifeboat to be lowered, leaving behind twenty-three of his men to fend for themselves. The ship was encased in a sheet of ice, and water was freezing into everything including the men. His wet, cold crew were lowering the lifeboat when one of the lines snapped, dumping the men into Lake Superior. Cold and wet, six of the men were pulled back aboard by their shipmates. Another managed to reach the lifeboat. The rest, including the captain, disappeared beneath the icy waves of Superior.

The *Kiowa* drifted along the shore, pulled by the storm. Arthur Kronk, the first mate, was now the acting captain. The crew was afraid and he tried to keep them calm as the situation worsened. Things weren't looking good for the crew. But on shore, someone saw the *Kiowa*'s situation.

Keeper Klaus Hamringa kept a personal journal and wrote of the wreck. In it he describes the events of the fateful night of the *Kiowa*. "On November 30, 1929, steamer *Kiowa* drifted 6 miles west of the light station, with a northwest gale. The crew launched a lifeboat, Saturday, which capsized, drowning five of the men. Everything on board the Kiowa was coated with ice, making it impossible to launch the boats. The steamer was on the side, stern down, with a 45 degree list. Mr. Chilson and two others were coming from a hunting trip west of the light station at 2 pm Sunday in a small gas boat, with rowboat in tow. Seeing the steamer they picked off three men, and made for the lighthouse, as the wind began to pick up from the northeast. The men were almost frozen:

> "We immediately sounded the whistle at 2 pm and gave danger signals for an hour or so. We could not see help coming, so we launched our gas boat. We started about dusk and it was dark when we arrived at the steamer Kiowa. Six men were accommodated in the gas boat, 5 in the row boat, and 5 in Chilson's boat. When we had the crew all off and were about a mile from the boat, following the shore line, making for a hunting camp about 4 miles from the station, we saw the light

of the Coast Guard boat coming. Flashing them signals, we ran alongside and put 16 of the crew on the Coast Guard boat which took them to Grand Marais."

Since the retirement of Captain Benjamin Trudell, a legendary figure in the Life Saving Service, the Grand Marais Coast Guard seemed to be not quite as efficient as they had been in the past. They had extra duties added to their routines as they became more and more assimilated into Coast Guard. Post World War I had seen the entrance of things like the fear of enemy submarines in the Great Lakes. The Coast Guard had brought in ships like Submarine Chasers into Lake Superior.

When Au Sable Lighthouse signaled for aid with the wreck of the *Kiowa*, the Coast Guard did not respond as quickly as they had in the past. The Coast Guard crews had been working on a submarine telephone cable when the Au Sable whistle blew. The Coast Guard reports say they dropped the repair job and responded to the distress call promptly.

Keeper Hamringa's journal doesn't bear that out. Neither does his entry in the light station log, "Sunday about 2 P.M. a boat came to station telling us that a boat got ashore last night, sometime between 7-8 P.M. Weather clear at the time. 5 men lost their lives. Started to sound signal for Coast Guard at 2 P.M. Did not come till dark. Sent 1st asst in station out with gas boat and row . All so the hunting party in their gas boat got the crew of 15 men before the Coast Guard hove in sight."

Supposedly they scrambled the lifeboat and headed for the light station at Au Sable, but why was it after dark before they appeared? Going overland was impossible as the blizzard had now deposited heavy wet snow into huge drifts. They claim they stopped at the Au Sable Lighthouse and learned from the keeper that the Kiowa was on shore west of Au Sable.

If the Coast Guard spoke with anyone it would have had to have been one of the wives. The two Assistant Keepers had accompanied Hamringa to assist with their own rescue after Chilson had deposited the first load of the Kiowa's crew and gone back a second time for more and removed a second load of the crew, before they encountered the Coast Guard.

The Coast Guard log about the incident is detailed in all aspects except in how they removed the crew from the Kiowa. It gives the impression that the Coast Guard rescued all of the Kiowa's crew, by stating "removed all 16 of the remaining crew safely," saying nothing about the part Chilson, his hunting buddies and Hamringa and his assistants played in saving what was left of the crew.

A Grand Marais fishing tug, the *Josephine Addison*, saw a lifeboat floating in the water. It was the lifeboat from the *Kiowa*. The one man who had managed to climb aboard was still on it. He was frozen, encased in ice. He was the sixth fatality of the Kiowa.

The portion of the crew who had been dropped at the lighthouse were still there. The Coast Guard didn't return for them immediately because another steamer, the George H. Donovan, was in trouble and they had to make a run out to her. They piloted her into the harbor and it was saved.

It was another day before they could get back to Au Sable to pick up the rest of the crew. Chilson and his two hunting partners were still there as well, and they went back to Grand Marais. In the bad weather the harbor had frozen and they had to break the ice to get back into the bay.

The Kiowa was one of the worst wrecks in the area and shipwreck historians have debated whether the Grand Marais Coast Guard had "missed" the rescue and tried to "gloss" over the mistake with the report.

Lightkeeper Hamringa and his two assistants, John R. Hamann and William Campbell, received commendations for the assistance they lent to the crew of the *Kiowa*. If it weren't for them, and of course Chilson and his hunting *partners*, the unsung heroes of the rescue, the loss of life would have been much higher. Again Hamringa had come through for those in distress. He retired two weeks later after a lifetime of distinguished service with another commendation from the Lighthouse Service. Heroes shine when heroes are needed.

When the need arises, heroes show themselves. They rise up unknowing to themselves and do what has to be done, regardless of their own safety and wellbeing. Heroes, they surround us today as they have in our past, and every day, another is revealed.

4   Lost Bonanza

This is a tale of exploration, of hardship, of discovery, and of shattered lost hopes in the Lake Superior region of Michigan. It's a story of rivalry and friendship. It is also a true story, one that takes you back to the dreams that settled and brought the intrepid to the wild, untamed north country and provided the foundations for what the Upper Peninsula of Michigan was to become.

In the mid and late 1800s, vast riches of minerals were discovered throughout the Upper Peninsula. Fortunes were amassed by many and the attraction drew countless with the hope of being the next one to make a major strike. It was just this that inspired three men to set out to explore an area of Marquette County that at the time was virtually untouched by white men. A few of the more prominent geologist explorers like Douglas Houghton and John Burt had gone through the area but other than that it was untraveled and unsettled. A mining captain of repute named Martin Daniels, his companions, John Tebo, and Sam York, set out from Marquette in 1897, north to the Sauks Head Lake area. Mounted on horses with a string of pack mules trailing behind them, they journeyed through the huge virgin pine and hardwoods, skirting the monster outcroppings of rock, ever wary of the wolves, bears, and cougars that freely roamed the wilderness.

Gold had been discovered north of Ishpeming (as evidenced by the Ropes and the Michigan Fire Gold Mines) and traces of gold, copper, and silver were found on Mount Mesnard, south of Marquette. All around Marquette, discoveries were being made and Daniels and his companions were certain that to the north would be no exception. There had been speculation on the possibilities for years previous in mining circles, but its inaccessibility made its overall cost infeasible. The trio wanted to prove otherwise.

They searched the wilderness while living in tents, and acquired their food by hunting and fishing, year around, rarely returning to

Marquette and their families. They chipped rock and dug test shafts. They suffered through every kind of weather that Lake Superior could throw at them. The life that they had chosen for themselves wasn't an easy one.

The next spring, in 1898, their efforts bore fruit. Martin Daniels brought back ore samples rich in copper. Once again that familiar mineral was discovered in the U.P. This time there came a twist. When Capt. Daniels returned in the fall, the ore not only carried large concentrations of copper, but also, there was considerable silver and yes, gold! Daniels had little trouble hiring ten more men to work what he called the "Franklin A" mine, named after Daniels' youngest child and the initials of John Tebo's youngest sister.

The news was anything but a secret and several adventurers set out for the area, searching for riches, creating a small Sauks Head gold rush. But, the trio had prepared for this. They had purchased all of the surrounding area of their claim. Besides being known for locating mineral deposits like a bloodhound, Martin Daniels was known for his business aptitude too, so he tried to anticipate everything he could.

While in Marquette on that fall trip, he also set up a company called the Sauks Head Mining Ventures. All accounts were set up and he made arrangements for the printing of stocks as a means of financing his endeavors.

To the west of Daniels' diggings was a true rarity for that area, a homestead, owned by the Krieg family on the Big Garlic River. The news of the Daniels discoveries prompted them to start their own explorations. Test shafts of their own were sunk in 1899. Their strike was announced, and also led to the formation of a company of their own called the Sauks Head Copper Mining and Development Company. Frank Krieg was superintendent and John Krieg came from Detroit to help work it.

A rivalry ensued between the Daniels and the Krieg mines. Both sent back regular reports on their progress and the quality of ore produced. Each were selling stock in their operations in attempts to raise funds. The Kriegs sold theirs to interested parties in Detroit for 25 cents a share while Martin Daniels sold his to Marquette and area residents for 50 cents each. Both mines had to ship their ore overland by wagons to the mouths of the Little and Big Garlic Rivers where there was always a race to obtain shipping space on the occasional ship that would anchor offshore.

Fig. 4-1: This the only picture of the Krieg Mine that I have ever seen. It also shows some of the surrounding mine buildings.

1902 saw both mines in peak production. Gold, silver and copper were all of the finest quality and appeared to be in larger abundance than either company had hoped in the beginning. The deeper each mine went, the wider and purer the veins got. Martin Daniels and Frank Krieg both commented freely on how they thought they had struck upon the richest deposits in the U.P.

A mine inspector named Joseph Tregonning who visited both mines that year concurred with these boasts. He said that the veins probably ran for miles and upon inspection said that the vein was nine feet wide at the Daniels site and was twelve feet wide at the Krieg site. He claimed that it was a good possibility that it was the identical vein that the Ropes Gold Mine had tapped. Tregonning stated that "There is no doubt that there is a bonanza at Sauks Head."

December 1902 saw a reorganization of the Daniels mine. Money was becoming scarce and when Martin tried to sell stocks, it was difficult because of the similarities of names between the companies. Prospective buyers weren't sure anymore which mine they were buying into. Consequently he changed the name of his to The Original Sauks

Head Mine Limited. With the new name and some new loans, he invested in more equipment with all of the capital he could muster.

But, Daniels' luck had run out and in the summer of 1903, work was stopped. The difficulties of shipment, bringing the ore to the surface, coupled with the slowness of digging with hand tools finally strapped the finances into bankruptcy. With the abandonment, the shafts quickly filled with water and were never given another thought as to reopening or salvaging.

Meanwhile, the Kriegs were flourishing. They hadn't spread themselves quite so thin and were into a slightly richer vein than Daniels had been. Now with no more competition for stocks and shipping, production was pushed to the limit. Their shaft was down 120 feet and branching off. Optimism was intense. Plans for a stamp mill were drawn up and a new shaft house erected. Everybody was going to get rich.

As the work continued unabated, some of the workers struck into a large piece of stone and as it fell loose, the Big Garlic River rushed in. Struggling through fast rising waters, the wet and scrambling miners escaped safely, the mine being the only casualty. It was irreversibly flooded. This was the end of the Krieg Mine and any other attempt at a later time never materialized.

It was also the end of what could have been eventually an Upper Peninsula gold rush. But instead the entire story faded into obscurity like so many other stories in the U.P., a bonanza lost yet lying there still, waiting for the next adventurers to try their luck.

5   Starvation on Isle Royale: The Story of Angelique Mott

Many of us think that getting stranded on an island would be a good thing. We fantasize of the isolation, the "getting away from it all," but reality, especially in this story, can be a very different thing. In 1845, a woman named Angelique and her husband Charlie Mott were left on Isle Royale in July and were stranded there until the next Spring.

Their provisions consisted of a half-barrel of flour, six pounds of butter, and some beans. A supply boat had been promised them, but it never arrived. Thus began a story of survival and starvation that is unequaled in the annals of Lake Superior history. The story is told in Angelique's own words, and the survival of this story of survival is nearly a miracle. The time was 1845, when Lake Superior was an unsettled frontier. The only real settlements were on the Keweenaw Peninsula with Fort Wilkins and Sault Sainte Marie. All else was wilderness. The story as told by Angelique Mott:

"When I and my husband Charlie Mott were first married, we lived in La Pointe (Wisconsin). Mr. Douglas and Mr. Barnard and some other 'big bugs' from Detroit had come up there on the schooner *Algonquin*, looking for copper. From La Pointe, Charlie and I went over with them, on their invitation, to Isle Royale. After landing with the rest, I wandered a long way on the beach until I saw something shining in the water. It was a piece of mass copper. When I told the *Algonquin* people of it they were very glad and determined at once to locate it. They said, if Charlie and I would occupy it for them, Charlie should have $25 a month and I $5 a month to cook for him. Having agreed to the bargain, we returned to the Sault to lay in a good supply of provisions. There I first met Mendenhall, the man

Fig. 5-1: Engraving of Isle Royale circa the time that the Motts were stranded on the island.

who brought us into all this trouble. He said there was no need of carrying provisions so far up the lake and at so heavy of an expense as he had plenty of provisions at La Pointe. When we got to La Pointe, we found that this was not so. All we could get was a half barrel of flour (which we had to borrow from the mission), six pounds of butter that smelt badly and was white like lard, and a few beans. I didn't want to go to the island until we had something more to live on, and I told Charlie so, but Cyrus Mendenhall over-persuaded him. He solemnly promised him two things: First, that he would send a bateau with provisions in a few weeks; and then at the end of three months, he would be sure to come himself and take us away. So, very much against my will, we went to Isle Royale on the first of July.

"Having a bark canoe and a net, for a while we lived on fish, but one day, about the end of summer a storm came and we lost our canoe and soon our net was broken and good for nothing also. Oh, how we watched and watched and watched but no bateau ever came to supply us with food. No vessel ever came to take us away, neither Mendenhall's nor any other. When at last we found that we had been deserted and that we would have to spend the whole winter on the island, and that there would be no getting away until spring, I tell you such a thought was hard to bear, indeed. Our flour and butter and beans were gone. We couldn't catch any more fish. Nothing else seemed left to us but sickness, starvation and death itself. All we could do was eat bark, and roots and bitter berries that only seemed to make the hunger worse. Oh, sir, hunger is an awful thing. It eats you up so inside, and you feel so all gone, as if you must go crazy. If you could only see the holes I made around the cabin in digging for something to eat, you would think it must have been some wild beast. Oh God, what I suffered there that winter from that terrible hunger, grace help me. I only wonder how I ever lived through it.

"Five days before Christmas (for you may be sure we kept account of every day) everything was gone. There was not so much as a single bean. The snow had come down thick and heavy. It was bitter, bitter cold and everything was frozen as hard as a stone. We hadn't any snowshoes. We couldn't dig any roots. We drew our belts tighter and tighter, but it was no use, you can't cheat hunger, you can't fill up that inward craving that gnaws within you like a wolf.

"Charlie suffered from it even worse than I did. As he grew weaker and weaker, he lost all heart and courage. Then, fever set in. It grew higher and higher until at last he went clear out of his head. One day he sprang up and seized his butcher knife and began to sharpen it on a whetstone. 'He was tired of being hungry' he said, 'He would kill a sheep, something to eat he must have.' And then, he glared at me as if he thought nobody could read his purpose but himself. I saw that I was the sheep he intended to kill and eat. All day and all night long I watched him and kept my eyes on him, not daring to sleep, and expecting him to spring upon me at any moment, but at last I managed to wrest the knife from him and that danger was over.

"After the fever fits were gone and he came to himself, he was as kind as ever and I never thought of telling him what a dreadful thing he had tried to do. I tried hard not to have him see me cry as I sat behind him, but sometimes I couldn't help it, as I thought of our hard lot, and saw him sink away and dry up until there was nothing left of him but skin and bones. At last he died so easily that I couldn't tell just when the breath did leave his body.

"This was another big trouble. Now that Charlie was dead, what could I do with him? I washed him and laid him out, but I had no coffin for him. How could I bury him when all around it was either rock or ground frozen as hard as rock? And I could not bear to throw him out into the snow. For three days I remained with him in the hut, and it seemed almost like company to me, but I was afraid that if I continued to keep up the fire, he would spoil. The only thing I could do was leave him in the hut where I could sometimes see him, and go off and build a lodge for myself and take my fire with me. Having sprained my arm in nursing and lifting Charlie, this was very hard work, but I did it at last.

"Oh that fire, you don't know what company that was. It seemed alive just like a person with you, as if it could almost talk, and many a time, but for its bright and cheerful blaze that put some spirits in me, I think I would have just died. One time I made too big a fire and almost burned myself out, but I had plenty of snow handy and so saved what I had built with so much labor and took better care for the future.

"Then came another big trouble, ugh, what a trouble it was, the worst trouble of all. You ask me if I wasn't afraid when thus left alone on the island. Not of the things you speak of. Sometimes it would be so light in the north, and even way up overhead like a second sunset, that the night seemed turned into day, but I was used to the dancing spirits and was not afraid of them. I was not afraid of the Mackee Monedo or Bad Spirit, for I had been brought up better at the mission than to believe all the stories that the Indians told about him. I believed that there was a Christ and that he would carry me through if I prayed to him. But the thing that most of all I was afraid of, and that I had to pray hardest against was this: Sometimes I was so hungry, so very hungry, and the hunger raged so in my veins that I was tempted, O, how terribly was I tempted to take Charlie and make soup of him. I knew it was wrong. I felt it was wrong. I didn't want to do it, but some day the fever might come on me as it did on him, and when I came to my senses I might find myself in the very act of eating him up. Thank God, whatever else I suffered, I was spared that, but I tell you of all the other things, that was the thing of which I was most afraid and against which I prayed the most and fought the hardest.

"When the dreadful thought came over me, or I wished to die, and die quick, rather than suffer any longer, and I could do nothing else, then I would pray, and it always seemed to me after praying hard something would turn up, or I would think of something that I had not thought of before and have new strength given me to fight it out still longer. One time in particular I remember, not long after Charlie's death, and when things were at their very worst. For more than a week I had nothing to eat but bark, and how I prayed that night that the good God would give me something to eat, lest the ever increasing temptation would come over me at last. The next morning when I opened the door, I noticed for the first time some rabbit tracks. It almost took away my breath and made my blood run through my veins like fire. In a moment I had torn a lock of hair out of my head and was plaiting strands to make a snare for them. As I set it, I prayed that I might catch a fat one and catch him quick. That very day I caught one, and so raging hungry was I that I tore off his skin and ate him up raw. It was nearly a week before I caught another, and so it was often for weeks together. The thing seemed so very strange to me that though I had torn half the hair out of my head to make snares, never once during the whole winter did I catch two rabbits at one time.

"Oh how heavily did the time hang upon me. It seemed as if the old moon would never wear out and the new one never come. At first I tried to sleep all that I could but after a while I got into such a state of mind and body that I could scarcely get any sleep night or day. When I sat still for an hour or two my limbs were so stiff and dried up that it was almost impossible for me to move them at all. So at last, like a bear in a cage, I found myself walking all the time. It was easier to walk than to do anything else. When I could do nothing else to relieve my hunger I would take a pinch of salt. Early in March I found a canoe that had been cast ashore and which I mended and made fit for use. Part of the sail I cut up and made the strips into a net. Soon the little birds began to come and I knew that spring was coming in good earnest. God indeed had heard my prayer and I felt I was saved. Once more I could see my mother.

"One morning in May I had good luck fishing and caught no less than four mullets at one time. Just as I was cooking them for breakfast I heard a gun, and I fell back almost fainting. Then I heard another gun and I started to run down to the landing but my knees gave way and I sank to the ground. Another gun and I was off to the boat in time to meet the crew when they came ashore. The very first man that landed was Mendenhall and he put up his hand to shake hands with me which I did. 'Where is Charlie?' said he. I told him he was asleep. He might go up to the hut and see for himself. Then they all ran off together. When Mendenhall went into the hut he saw that Charlie was dead. The men took off Charlie's clothes and shoes and saw plain enough that I had not killed him but that he had died of starvation. When I came up Mendenhall began to cry and to try to explain things. He said that 'he had sent off a bateau with provisions and didn't see why they didn't get to us.' But the boys told me it was all a lie. I was too glad to get back to my mother to do anything. I thought his own conscience ought to punish him more than I could do."

Angelique Mott was a large Native American woman who had grown up in her tribe and was well equipped with forest lore and outdoor survival skills. It is a well documented fact that many trappers were shown by the natives that one could survive from cooked poplar/aspen bark for quite a while. Angelique lived until 1874 and died in Sault Ste. Marie. To display how strong she was, there is a story that says a Frenchman made her a bet that she couldn't carry a barrel of pork to the top of a nearby hill and back. She won it with ease and when she finished she volunteered to carry the barrel up again, but this time with the Frenchman on top of it.

Author's Note: The transcription of Angelique Mott's story is taken from a footnote. Yeah, you read that right, the entire story is a footnote in the first printing of a book called *The Honorable Peter White* by Ralph D. Williams in 1907. The first printing of this book has a huge number of footnotes that run on for pages with stories and information surrounding the main subject of the book. In later editions of this book, many of the footnotes were purged including this story. I felt that Angelique Mott and her story stand as a testament to the strength of women and should be told once more.

6   The One-Time Train

Between the towns of Champion and Michigamme, in Michigan's Upper Peninsula, the Peshekee River flows into Lake Michigamme. It is an exceptionally beautiful river that cuts through Upper Peninsula mountains and deep forests. When seen, it is easy to understand why the wealthy McCormick family chose the area as the location for their wilderness getaways and Michigan's moose transplant project chose as the best possible area for success. Running north off from M-28, just past the bridge that crosses the Peshekee when traveling west, a small blacktop road meanders along the river. The road is called the

Fig. 6-1: The ore dock that was built at Huron Bay. Only a few pilings in Lake Superior are all that remains today.

Peshekee Grade and leads to the famed McCormick Tract, a large section of land once owned by Cyrus McCormick. Most people know that this road was built over the top of a former railroad grade, hence the name, but the story of that particular railroad is one of a kind and rarely told.

In late 1889, a project was proposed and adopted by owners of the Champion mines and several other interested private investors. At the mouth of the Slate River, which empties into Huron Bay in northeast Baraga County, there was about to come into existence an immense ore dock. Its completion was only a matter of months. The dock contained two million feet of lumber and three thousand pilings. It was built to handle the shipping from a slate quarry which was in operation in a town called Arvon situated about four miles to the south. The Champion mine owners and investors decided that it would be immensely profitable for them to build their own railroad to the Huron Bay ore dock. At the time, their entire product was being handled by the Duluth South Shore and Atlantic Railroad, which took it to Marquette and shipped it from there. Shipping their ore themselves would eliminate this cost plus open up the Huron Mountain range for further mineral and lumber development. They were optimistic of obtaining all shipping business that would come out of the area. They were already certain of the Arvon quarry using the line along with a few lumbering operations that were currently under way.

Plans were drawn and money was invested in what they called the Iron Range and Huron Bay Railroad. It was decided that the railroad should be laid alongside the Peshekee River and then as it splits into tributaries, the railbed would move away and follow the Slate River to the Huron Bay.

Bids were called for from local contractors through the regional newspapers by a man named Milo Davis, the Chief Engineer and Superintendent of Construction. The main office for the railroad was set up in Arvon near the slate quarry. The bids were filed and they chose one by a contractor named Wallace Dingman, who, as it turned out, grossly underbid the project to secure the contract. He divided it up to several sub-contractors. Dingman also assured the company that the project would be complete in little over a year.

Construction began in 1890 and because of the rough terrain, the grade was a master engineering feat. Several low areas had to be filled in with rock for support. The trestles of heavy cedars and massive pine.

Fig. 6-2: This rock cut that shows the overwhelming scope of human endeavor that it took to build the railroad.

were erected on top of these. The longest of these contained over five hundred feet of rock fill and a mile of trestle

Another major construction obstacle was the huge rock outcroppings that are so abundant in the area. Several rock cuts had to be made through the high bluffs. The rock strata of the area is of the Canadian Shield, which consists of the hardest granites there is. The largest of these cuts was located near Arvon and was necessary if the railroad was to follow the Slate River down to the bay. Literally tons of black powder, steam drills to place the charges and large crews of workmen were required to move the forty thousand cubic yards of rock that it took to make the cut. This created a divide at an altitude of 1,960 feet. The work was so intensive that a camp was set up with several log buildings and partially underground huts that were constructed on the site. Even a blacksmith shop was required. This one cut alone cost $500,000.

This wasn't all it cost. It took three years to complete and it cost many lives. Because of the mostly underground living quarters and a shortage of supplies, typhoid broke out. The results were horrible. The scene was medieval, like when one pictures the plague. Dr. Paul Van Riper of Champion, years later, remarked on it. "There was a great many died. How many, I have no way of knowing. The Champion Hospital was filled as well as the house next door. They were also hauled to Ishpeming by team. The wagon used to come up at night and haul away the dead nearly every night." Milo Davis watched his crew sicken and die around him, yet he pressed on with the construction.

Dingman, when he underbid, expected the company to pick up the excess no matter what expenses incurred. Almost immediately he ran over-budget. The Iron Range and Huron Bay only paid him his bid amount. After so much the company refused to pay anymore. Consequently Dingman ran out of money and couldn't pay the subcontractors. Everybody owed everybody money.

Costs had soared. It was so expensive that at one point in 1891, work was stopped because there was no money to pay the workers. In Michigamme and Champion they lined the railroad platforms angrily, calling for the paymaster. Some workers were paid in time checks, which were in turn bought up in some communities at a 50% discount. Some paychecks had been outstanding for several months and merchants all along the line from L'anse, Michigamme, Champion and Marquette who had accepted the checks or extended credit to workers were suddenly finding themselves in near financial ruin. Daily, workers lined the railroad platforms waiting for the pay that was to come on the train from Detroit. Wallace Dingman, was forced to mortgage his property for $10,000 to cover pay for his workers.

At one point, Milo Davis was called into court to answer for expenses of food, blankets and supplies to keep men working and alive during the typhoid attack. The courts made him out to be frivolous and not having the authority to keep the crews supplied. He was raked over the coals thoroughly by the lawyers.

Finally the investors were able to get more backing through loans and the money came once again. Work resumed and the line was completed in 1893, without Dingman. A small settlement was even erected at the site of the ore dock in anticipation of the business boom that was to come. All in all, approximately two million dollars was spent in constructing 45 miles of track and purchasing two locomotives and 21 flatcars.

A former hotel proprietor from L'anse named Sam Beck worked as a railroad watchman. He told newspaper reporters about the first trip on the new railroad. "The engines were unloaded from the boats at

Fig. 6-3: Iron Range & Huron Bay railroad engine. It ran once before flying off the tracks on its maiden run.

Huron Bay. As the last eleven miles of the road was downgrade, it was decided to make a test run." The engine was fired and Beck climbed into the cab
with the engineer. "We had proceeded up the grade when the roadbed gave away and we went into the ditch." The engine lay in the Peshekee.

It was the one and only time a train traveled the railway. The loans that the Iron Range and Huron Bay Railroad had laden themselves with were immediately called in. Unable to pay, the bankrupt investors sold all they had. The locomotive was pulled from the Peshekee River where it lay and sold along with the other unused one along with the flatcars to the Algoma Central Railroad. The rails were pulled up and sold to the Detroit Urban Railroad. The whole project turned out to be disaster for all concerned. $2,000,000 worth of railroad was sold for $110,000.

Milo Davis, went to Detroit where lawsuits began catching up to him. He lost most of the money he'd made from those suits. Probably thinking that he would become the corporate scapegoat in upcoming suits in the Upper Peninsula, he went to Mexico. Having seen so many men die and then lawsuits flying everywhere while never having any luck in previous court experiences, a change of scenery was what he chose and was never heard from again. The U.P. newspapers vilified him as an embezzler and a cheat, a fugitive from justice.

The slate quarries in Arvon ceased soon after. The little settlement at the ore dock continued for a short time but was burned down by an Indian woman who was angry at a storekeeper. The remains of the ore dock were then dismantled in February 1901.

In the end nothing remained of the Iron Range and Huron Bay Railroad except an empty roadbed and some shattered dreams. It was a one-time train that never carried a single pound of cargo.

7 Grand Marais:
Surviving on the Shore of Superior

Fig. 7-1 : Grand Marias as it appeared as it wrapped around the bay.

"A place most delightful and wondrous for its nature that made it so pleasant to the eye and spirit," wrote Pierre Esprit Raddison in 1658 about Grand Marais. Since then, the community on the Lake Superior shore has seen many changes and transitions, but Raddison's impression of the Grand Marais harbor and its surrounding area still holds true. "Nature in abundance" the sign proclaims as one enters the quiet village.

It appears that as long as there has been human life around Lake Superior, Grand Marais harbor was a place of safety and a source of sustenance. Its isolated location made it a prime place to flee danger on the water and weather a storm along Lake Superior's south eastern shoreline. This section of water is known as "the shipwreck graveyard" and is considered one of the most dangerous areas in the world to sail. Grand Marais' kidney-shaped bay naturally protects from rough water.

The unique environment of the Grand Marais area makes it a source of a variety of things. Cold streams provide trout. Fields of blueberries and pockets of wild leeks are plentiful. Hardwood and conifer forests provided large stands of birch and cedar. These are all essential ingredients for the lifestyle of the Native American. It is the setting of Native legends and is considered a sacred area.

When the French explorers first came through, it is believed they stopped there, possibly as early as 1619. There are no actual written accounts before Radisson's in 1658. This makes it one of the oldest place names in the U.S.

The name Grand Marais literally translates to "the Great Marsh." There is no great marsh in the immediate region. On an occasional early French map it is shown as "le Grand Mare" meaning a large harbor. In French "Mare" and "Marais" are pronounced the same. The possibility exists that Marais is some map makers error that through repetition came to stick.

A permanent settlement began in 1830. A trading post was established near the mouth of the Sucker River in what has become known as East Bay. Over the years a settlement grew around it. Its growth prompted the west bay to be platted in 1852.

Soon, like most places in the U.P., its rich resources made it a prime place for exploitation. Its natural harbor, of course, enhanced its shipping viability and Grand Marais became a thriving community. Sawmills, shipping and commercial fishing dominated as the local industries.

Grand Marais's harbor was strategically important for all other shipping on the lakes as well being the only harbor along this section of shore. The violence of the storms on the east end of the lake made the harbor a place of safety, a refuge for ships in trouble. A breakwall was constructed in 1872. A lifesaving station was established in 1899 including lighthouse and lightkeeper's home. This was Grand Marais' boom years (Fig. 7-4).

In Grand Marais' peak years, more than 2,000 countable residents lived there. There were probably another thousand living in the lumber camps and surrounding woods. The town thrived and unlike many lumber towns, it was a family town. Many U.P. lumber towns were mostly men. Grand Marais was different. There were a large number of boarding houses, saloons and bordellos. Many relationships were developed here and new families were commonplace. Work abounded and there was no shortage of employment.

Grand Marais was a full-fledged town with doctors, lawyers, bankers, photographers, a hospital, social clubs, hotels, restaurants, department stores, livery stables, and churches. A train had a daily run

Fig. 7-2: Main Street in Grand Marais as it appeared before a fire destroyed most of it.

Fig. 7-3: A home of the huge lumber operations that thrived there.

Fig. 7-4: The legendary Grand Marais Lifesaving Station that rescued mariners from the teeth of Lake Superior

to Seney. The Protestants held their first church services on a boat in the harbor.

City water was introduced in 1896 at no charge to the residents. The original pipes were made of hollow wood. There was even a mill that generated electricity. It operated only during certain hours in the day. A man had to jump on the flywheel to get it started. Eventually it was turned over to the township and was in use until 1956.

The boom was short-lived though. Lumber companies had sprung up around the community with four situated on the shoreline. One was a veneer plant. Most of the lumber was being shipped out by rail or boat. Residents recall that there were sometimes as many as forty ships in the harbor at one time. Lots of money was being made on Grand Marais' resources, but unfortunately all of it was going back to Detroit. By 1910, all the lumber companies were on their way out. It was the year they closed the railroad.

Residents loaded up their belongings and rode the final trains for more prosperous places. In 1911, they took up the tracks. Grand Marais became isolated. The only way to reach it was by boat. There was no road. By 1915, there were only 200 residents left. Later that year there was a fire, which destroyed most of the buildings along Lake Street (Fig. 7-2).

The mid-1920s brought to Grand Marais a much needed road to Seney. It was after this that tourist cabins began to appear. Commercial fishing kept many families alive. A new high School was built in 1926. Blueberry picking and fern gathering were other meager incomes to be had.

One of the more interesting events that left a lasting impression on Grand Marais is the tale behind the acquisition of the town's most unusual building, the Pickle Barrel (currently used during the summer as a visitor's information center). It was built in 1926 as a gift for William Donahey, creator the famous Teeny Weenie children's characters. The characters were originally drawn for the Chicago Tribune and were featured for many years in the children's Highlights magazine. Donahey had allowed his characters to be used to promote a line of pickles for the Monarch food line. As a gift for his wife, author Mary Dickerson Donahey, he had a life-size replica of the pickle barrel constructed on the north shore of Grand Sable Lake. It was their summer home for ten years and then it was moved into town. It has remained as Grand Marais' most unusual landmark and one of the first things a traveler to Grand Marais sees when arriving into town. Donahey is also significant as the donor of the land that became Woodland Park.

The single modern event that has changed Grand Marais is the creation of Pictured Rocks National Lakeshore in 1966. The U.S. Park Service bought property all around Grand Marais, stretching to Munising. All residences around Grand Sable Lake were bought or condemned and destroyed. Camping facilities, scenic overlooks, and public accesses were developed, which invited tourists to the area. Grand Marais remains to this day a tourist destination that is continually growing as more and more are discovering the area.

Grand Marais is a thriving community. It is a summer getaway for tourists and a retreat for artists of all kinds. The area's beauty infects most visitors. It is a place of quiet and serenity, where nature's dramas are played out to their unpredictable ends.

New summer homes are constructed every year.

The harbor now sees recreational sailboats instead of cargo ships carrying their loads of lumber. The beaches are for sunbathers and agate hunters. Grand Marais remains an important harbor of refuge, but the harbor currently needs upkeep. There has been virtually no maintenance on the Grand Marais breakwater in 100 years, though the pier itself was worked on by the Army Corps of Engineers in 1950. The real problem is that a breakwall swept completely across the harbor. The top of it is no longer visible above Lake Superior. It is a hazard to boats. The other problem stems from the Sucker River, which drains into the harbor. Through the year it carries tons of silt into the bay. Because of the breakwall, all of that silt is slowly filling it up. The harbor needs to be dredged badly. Soon we may see the extinction of an age-old harbor. By man's alteration and now neglect, there will no longer be a place of safety along the most dangerous coast in the Great Lakes.

A visit to the Grand Marais Lighthouse Keeper's House Museum is needed, to get an idea of Grand Marais' early days,. Located alongside the harbor breakwall, it is like going into someone's house. "Most of the people who come here are really interested in the history of the area. They linger and take their time, asking questions and learning about Grand Marais," comments Donna Oglevie, one of the museum's curators. "This way we get to know them and many return over and over."

The museum is only open during peak summer months, but then it's seven days. It is completely operated by volunteers. There is no admission charge though donations are greatly appreciated.

The museum was acquired in 1984 and opened in '85. The exhibits were sparse, but over the years many donations have come to the historical society. The Lighthouse keeper's house is now well stocked with memories and items of the past. The two-story building has every room full of displays. "We like to make the museum interesting for kids," says Oglevie. "We have things to let them touch."

The Grand Marais Historical Society has approximately 20-30 members.

"This is very rewarding," says Oglevie. "Occasionally we get a former resident who comes in here. They help us piece together the things that we weren't aware of. One lady told us what the house (the lighthouse keeper's house) used to look like. Another was a man who had lived there as a child."

For more information on the Grand Marais Historic Society or the museum, write to Grand Marais, or call 906-494-2306

8 George Shiras III: Photography by Camera and Flashlight

"I see. You know George Shiras three. He must be very interesting."

"He is. He's about the most interesting man I know."

—Ernest Hemingway, "Homage to Switzerland" (1932)

George Shiras III (or as Shiras signed it, "*3d*") first saw the woods and waters of northern Michigan in the summer of 1870, when he was 11 years old on a trip to Marquette with his father. Nothing in his later experience would ever dim the impression they made on him—not the trappings of wealth and position; not the influence of the finest schools; not the example of his father, a U.S. Supreme Court justice; not a promising legal career of his own. Not even a term spent in the U.S. Congress, where he introduced the legislation that would become the Migratory Bird Law—securing for Shiras an important place in the annals of conservation—could lure him away for long.

Shiras returned every summer to Marquette for over 70 years. There he married his wife, daughter of Peter White, and had two children, a boy and a girl. During his early years, the interests of George Shiras 3d were those of a keen hunter and fisherman. As he grew older and his viewpoint broadened, he became more and more enthralled by the wildlife and the beauties of the region where he had passed so many years. By the late 1880s his hunting instincts had been more and more replaced by the sympathetic desire of the naturalist to know more of the lives, habits, and mentality of the wild things he so often encountered. Whatever that quality was, by 1889, his 30th year, he largely laid gun and rod aside in favor of a more absorbing instrument: the camera.

Shiras' own words:

Fig. 801: This shows Shiras' camera setup as he floated down a river catching pictures of wildlife in the night.

"Fairly within the realm of romance were my two days travel on foot, with an Indian guide, when I was twelve years old, through a pristine wilderness to a beautiful lake hidden in the forest about twenty miles east of Marquette. The lake had been discovered by my guide the year before. I named it Whitefish Lake because a small river of that name entered Lake Superior at a point that made probable its origin in this lake, although this connection was not verified until a few years later. To this secluded place I have returned for more than sixty consecutive years, first as a boy and later often accompanied by relatives and friends. The natural beauties of this woodland haven and the interesting wildlife inhabiting the surrounding forest undoubtedly had a governing influence in developing my career as a sportsman-naturalist. It was there that, as a youthful hunter, I shot my first deer. There I took my first daylight And flashlight photographs of wildlife, and there I became an observing field naturalist."

Whitefish Lake (now known as Peter White Lake) near Deerton, became the family retreat. It was a place that would soon go down in the annals of photographic history as the location for Shiras' innovative and pioneering wildlife photography. Wildlife photography barely existed: Cameras were cumbersome and primitive, wildlife was elusive and difficult to film. But Shiras's inventive genius contrived methods and devices that resulted, among other things, in the first flash photographs and the first trip-wire photography of animals at night. Other photographers of the day had captured breathtaking scenes of landscapes and wars, portraits of people and individuals, but wildlife was unexplored territory.

Shiras devised several methods of capturing wildlife on film. One, he would float quietly in a canoe after dark, his camera mounted on the front, intently listening until he heard noise or movement and then take a shot toward the source of the sound. Another was where he set up bait attached to trip wires where any animal taking the bait would also take its own picture. The results of some of these shots portrayed wildlife in never-before-seen images of the creatures of the wilderness going about their habits and routines. The mysteries of wildlife were presented to the world.

Shiras' pictures were breathtakingly dynamic, utterly unique for the times. Enlargements of some of them, the famous "Midnight Series" of deer at night, photographed entirely around Deerton, won the gold medal in the forestry division at the Paris Exposition of 1900 and then won top prize in the photographic division as well, without ever having been formally entered in that competition! The series also received the grand prize at the St. Louis World Fair in 1904. Perhaps inevitably, Shiras came to the attention of Gilbert H. Grosvenor, the Editor of *National Geographic*, with results that set the standard for the Geographic's photographic reputation. The July 1906 *National Geographic* published wildlife photographs by Shiras. Grosvenor printed 74 of them accompanied by only a brief text, devoting nearly the entire issue to George 3d, a proportion unheard of in its day. The gamble was wildly successful, making this issue of the magazine one of the most significant ever published. For Shiras, it meant wide dissemination of his pioneering work. For the National Geographic Society, it meant a gratifying surge in membership and the beginning of a close and renowned association with wildlife photography.

The impact of the July 1906 *National Geographic* reached all the way to the President Theodore Roosevelt, who was so taken that he

Fig. 10-2: Wildlife selfies - this is a raccoon taking its own picture through Shiras' tripwire method. This would also be the first trailcam.

Fig. 10-2: This is the famous beaver picture which Shiras shot. It is the first time ever that a beaver was caught on camera doing what it is most famous for. Theodore Roosevelt highly commended Shiras for this accomplishment.

Fig. 10-3: An example of Shiras' river photography. I personally own an original copy of this from Shiras' studio.

Fig. 10-4: Lynx captured on film in Loon Lake, Ontario

promptly picked up his pen and implored Shiras to "write a big book—a book of bulk as well as worth, in which you shall embody these pictures and the results of all your invaluable notes upon the habits, not only of game but of the numerous other wild creatures that you have observed....Do go ahead and do this work!" Shiras was deeply impressed with this appeal. But he was too busy in the active pursuit of photography and conservation work to undertake it at the time. For the next several decades he ranged all over North America with his cameras, but always returning to his beloved place at Whitefish Lake. All the while his relationship to the National Geographic Society strengthened. Between 1906 and 1932, Shiras published nine illustrated articles in the *National Geographic,* which generated so many requests for prints that pictorial supplements of two of his prizewinning photographs of deer at night were included with the July 1913 and August 1921 issues.

But as he grew older and his eyesight began to dim, Shiras recalled Roosevelt's insistence and resolved to finally write his "big book." Once again he turned to the Geographic. After all, he had been a Society trustee since 1911, and in 1928 he, in turn, entrusted 2,400 of his finest photographs to the Society for permanent retention in its files. Now he selected 950 of these images for inclusion in a two-volume work comprising extensively revised versions of his many articles.

Eventually Shiras was forced to set aside his camera. He ultimately produced a two-volume book about his wilderness photography titled *Hunting Wild Game with Camera and Flashlight.* This magnum opus was published in 1935, the first volume of which is almost entirely devoted to the images captured at Whitefish Lake and the Upper Peninsula. Nearly thirty years had elapsed since Roosevelt had first urged him to compile it, and in belated recognition of this inspiration, Shiras dedicated the volumes to the memory of the late President. It was very warmly received. The prestigious British Journal *Nature* echoed most reviews when it proclaimed the book "an outstanding work of its kind" that "must be looked upon as a classic in the history of wildlife photography."

Despite this reception, the exacting Shiras unhappily discovered that many minor errors had crept into the text. So despite failing health, for he was now 78, he labored to make the necessary corrections as quickly as possible. The result was the second edition of the work, amended, revised, and enlarged, published in 1936. Still unsatisfied,

Shiras even began work on a third edition, but did not finish it before he died in 1942 at 83. Thus it is the second edition, in Shiras's judgment, that is the better of the two. Summing up his own life's work as well as his relationship with the Society, its pages remain the most complete guide to the world of George Shiras, a world of woods and waters and wildlife. It remains a monument to an important early conservationist who is also known as "the original advocate of wildlife photography."

Thus George Shiras 3d, the original advocate of wildlife photography, was (1) the first to photograph in daytime wild animals of birds from a canoe or blind; (2) the first to get automatic daylight pictures of wild animals by their touching a string across a trail or pulling on bait attached to a string operating the shutter of a camera; (3) the first to operate the camera at a distance by a string running from a blind; (4) the first to invent a means for picturing animals from a canoe by hand flashlight; (5) the first to invent a means to obtain automatic flashlight photographs for which the animals or birds fired the flash; (6) the first to use two flashlights and two cameras, one set picturing the animal when quiescent and the other set, a second later, showing the animal in action when alarmed by the explosion of the first flashlight; and (7) the first to practice wing shooting with the camera by means of a specially devised apparatus by which wild fowl and shore birds can be photographed when flying from 50 to 70 miles an hour.

George Shiras 3d was one of the true pioneers of the Upper Peninsula. He realized its potential then took it to a historic level. His name still graces many places in the Marquette area, as it should. He revolutionized a medium that we take for granted every day. He was an amazing man for an amazing place.

Collectors note: The July 1906 *National Geographic* was so popular that it was reprinted soon after its initial publication. These reprints are apparently indistinguishable from the originals. Reprints were also made in 1964. These are marked "reprint" on the bottom of the cover. The pictorial supplements issued with the July 1913 and August 1921 issues came folded inside the front covers of the magazines. Both unfolded and framed copies were available upon written request to Society headquarters. As can be seen in the illustrations, it is clear that these reproductions were published by the Society. Shiras had approved a series of limited-edition bromide enlargements of his award-winning "Midnight" pictures in 1901, prior to his close involvement with the National Geographic Society. These were produced in a variety of sizes, often limited to a thousand copies apiece. "Copyright by George Shiras 3d" would probably appear in the lower left corner of each.

9   Stockades of Terror

AUTHOR'S NOTE: This piece of history is about a very dark part of the past. There are graphic passages that illustrate the depth of these stockades of terror. When I first came across these stories, I had a hard time believing them, but as I researched on, I realized not only was this widespread, but as I followed the thread of the story, I realized that it was all too tragically true. Different accounts when pieced together fit nicely into a picture of an organization of crime that ruled with an iron hand and cruelty that reached to the depths of cold inhumanity. BEWARE: This next section is not for the faint of heart.

In the late 1800s in Michigan's Upper Peninsula, an early group of organized crime set up a series of "stockades" that were located to serve logging camps and mining communities throughout the peninsula. These places were prostitution camps that kidnapped women and enslaved them using torturous methods of abuse and brainwashing. All of it was controlled by one man and woman, a pair that embodied evil incarnate.

This all starts with Chase S. Osborn and his book *The Iron Hunter*. The Hon. Chase Osborn holds the distinction of being the only governor of Michigan from the Upper Peninsula. Most of his life was spent in Sault Ste. Marie and he started the Sault Evening News newspaper. He wrote several books and was highly respected by his peers. In one of his books, *The Iron Hunter*, he talks about his early life as a newspaper man and his encounters with one of these infamous places.

Chase Osborn's account:

> "This took place at Florence, Wisconsin, in the heart of the Menominee iron range, one of the Lake Superior iron ore districts. Conditions here were similar to those of every new

Fig. 9-1: Chase S. Osborn as he appeared during his time as Michigan Governor. He was a newspaper man that helped expose the "stockades" in the late 1800's

range. There is always an outlaw headquarters in all new regions remote from disciplined centers. Florence, at this period of the early eighties (1880s) was a metropolis of vice. There was gambling on the main streets, outdoors in inclement weather and screened indoors when driven in by the cold and storms. Prostitution was just as bold. Its red passion garbings paraded every prominent place in town.

"A mile out of town, Mudge's stockade was the central supply station. It was the prison used by the nerviest white slavers that ever dealt in women. A big log camp with frame gables held a bar and dance hall and stalls on the first floor. On the second floor were rooms about the size of those in a Tokyo Yoshiwara. A third floor attic contained dungeons and two trap doors. In the cellar were dark cells and a secret passage, well timbered with cedar, leading to where the hill on which the stockade was located broke down into a dense swamp. Surrounding this camp of death, and worse, were sharp-pointed palisades, ten feet high, of the kind used against the Indians to inclose pioneer blockhouses. There were loopholes. Two passages led through the stockade. One was wide enough to admit a team. This was fastened with hornbeam cross bars. The other entrance was narrower and for commoner use. It was protected by a solid sliding gate of ironwood. On either side of this gate, inside, two big, gaunt, terrifying timber wolves were chained. This stockade was a wholesale warehouse of women.

"There were several in the Lake Superior iron country in the early days, but I think the one at Florence was the most notorious and the worst. It was built by 'old man' Mudge. He was a white-livered, sepulchral individual who wore a cotton tie, a Prince Albert coat and a plug hat; even wore this outfit when he fed the wolves. Mudge worked as a preacher through northern Indiana and Ohio and the scoundrel used his clerical makeup to fine advantage. He had a ready tongue and roped in girl after girl. Not much attention was paid in those days to pimping and procuring. Whenever a murder grew out of his acts, the old fox would so involve his trail that, if it led anywhere at all, a church was at the end of it, and that would throw off the sleuth.

"Old Mudge ruined his daughter Mina, and she was 'Keeper' of the place. Mina Mudge was a stunning woman. Her concentrated depravity, for she too had a child and brought it up in infamy, was glossed over by a fine animal figure, a rubescent complexion, semi-pug nose, lurking gray eyes, sensual lips and sharpish chin. Her lips were the clew to passion, and eyes and chin betokened the cruelty of a she hyena. Girls were wheedled or beaten into submission, and nearly always when she sold them she had them broken to the business."

Chase Osborn's detailed descriptions of these stockades of terror allow for an in-depth picture of not only the criminals behind the operations, but allow for a look inside these operations that were prevalent throughout the 1880s Upper Peninsula. As Osborn continues his narration of his days in Florence, He not only describes more of the terror, but also makes ties into other events in the history of the U.P. as being instigated by Mudge and his gang. These accusations will be detailed in the next section.

More from Osborn:

"In the evening, a shrinking, girlish young woman was found just outside our door by my wife. She cowered and shivered and looked wild-eyed. It took some time to coax her in. After warmth and food, she told her story. Old Mudge had found her on a farm in Ohio. An orphan, she was sort of bound out, and her life was one of work and little else. Rather attractive, she was spied by the old serpent, and taken north 'to a good home.' Mina Mudge starved her, beat her, tied her ankles and wrists with thongs and, to break her in with terror, fastened her just out of reach of the wolves. It was night and the girl grew cold with exposure and fear. Her wrists and ankles shrunk some. And she wriggled out of the cutting thongs. Then she fled to the swamp and hid until hunger forced her to search for food.

We took as good care of her as our means afforded and planned her complete rescue. The girl disappeared. It was years later before I knew what had befallen her. Mudge's gang had located and trapped her. They forcibly kidnapped her and carried her to the wolf stockade. There she was given no chance to escape. Her spirit was broken. She was sold to a brothel keeper in Ontonagon County, Michigan, and was murdered by him one night in a ranch near to the Lake Superior shore. Murders often occurred, but those guilty were seldom punished. When this girl so mysteriously disappeared from my house, I was suspicious. I went to the sheriff, an Irish saloon-keeper, but I could not get him to act. He was either a member of the gang or honestly afraid."

"The Mudge gang was organized over a territory including the region for five hundred miles south of Lake Superior from Canada to Minnesota. Mudge was as much of a genius in some directions as he was a devil in others. They did not confine themselves to woman stealing. They would run off witnesses when arrests occurred near the law-and-order line. If they could not get rid of them any other way, the witnesses were killed. Any man who showed an inclination to oppose the gang was either intimidated or murdered. Within their own ranks a rebel never got away alive. Mudge tolerated no rivals. The most notorious murder he was responsible for was that of Dan Dunn, at Trout Lake. Dunn was just as bad a man as Mudge, and not much of a sneak about it. That was really how Mudge came to get him."

There will be more on the Dan Dunn murder later in this piece. Osborn was sent to Florence to get a newspaper up and running. The previous editor and owner had mysteriously disappeared. It fell on Osborn to take it over which made him an immediate target for the Mudge gang. Osborn and his family were now in constant danger and the harder he pushed, the more imminent the danger was.

Osborn continues:

"The gang was against all newspapers and dead against any that tried to improve conditions or oppose them in any way. Just a little time before they had burned the *Manistique Pioneer* office and had tried desperately but unsuccessfully to assassinate its brave editor, the late Major Clarke, a veteran of the Civil War. All along the line they had terrorized editors if possible. So the first night after I arrived they shot out my windows and shot a leg off one of the job presses, just to show me what they would do to me if I wasn't 'good'."

Stockades similar to what Osborn describes in the previous passages were prevalent across Michigan's Upper Peninsula. In researching this subject, I have been able to confirm the existence of several of these stockades. Seney, Sac Bay, Ewen, Trout Creek, Ontonagon, Bruce Crossing, all have been confirmed. He mentions several more, which are probably true as well, but the ones above definitely existed. Osborn fortunately gives enough information in his narrative, that to look deeper into his accusations is possible. The one in Ontonagon was located directly across from what is now the Ontonagon Township Campground on Lake Superior. One cannot help but think about the girl Osborn tried to save and was shipped to Ontonagon County along Lake Superior. I was able to confirm this through the Ontonagon Historical Society who even helped me find its former location. When the Ontonagon Stockade was eventually run out, it is said by local sources that it moved operations to Bruce Crossing, thirty miles south.

In the book *The Ontonagon Country*, James K. Jamison writes about Ewen and Ontonagon, "Ewen was a typical frontier town in a different and much later era than Ontonagon when the latter was a typical frontier town. Ontonagon was half a century old when crude, jerry built Ewen slapped together its first bare frame buildings in the pine boom. Ewen became substantial, respectable when the pine was gone."

"Chase Osborn, destined to become governor of the state, was a young moral crusader in the terrific mining camp at Florence, just over the state line in Wisconsin. He battled the corrupting elements of the place so vigorously in his little weekly newspaper that he had to transact business along the sprawling main street with a loaded Winchester rifle across his arm. One particularly notorious keeper of houses of ill fame, Osborn drove out of the community. Forced to find another field of social endeavor, this man moved his chattels to the hustling little town of Ewen."

"But if Ewen was rough, tough and ready, so also was Ontonagon, but perhaps with a little more decorum. Ewen was a wild youth. Ontonagon was middle-aged. Ontonagon's bartenders went in for fancy vests, waxed mustaches and fast driving horses. It had a big brick department store and a new brick courthouse. It had a main street devoted to business pursuits six or seven blocks long and one could pass along it and find stores sandwiched between the saloons. But it felt the surge of the tide from the logging camps on many an occasion. Out east of town a mile on the lake shore, glamour girls entertained in an enclosure known as 'The Stockade.' Cautious lumberjacks deliberately bent on getting uproariously drunk, made preliminary preparations by asking their friends, the saloon keepers, to put part of their stakes in the saloon safes. Presently there would be nothing left, or that is to say, it was all there but the ownership had changed."

"It is the style now for young writers to say that the 'Stockade' of early lumber towns was fiction. Dr. Covert (wrote a book called *Glory of the Pines* based on his observations in the Ontonagon country, now long out of print) and Chase Osborn are good witnesses that they did exist. Thirty years ago the ruins of the Ontonagon Stockade were plainly visible."

The Night of Vigilantes—the Sac Bay Stockade

One of the more detailed accounts of one of the stockades comes from an early history source, the *History of Fayette and Fairbanks Township* by Adele Elliot. Ms. Elliot was a long-time resident of the Garden Peninsula at Fayette. Sac Bay was located about six miles south of Fayette and was the site of one of the stockades. This is how she puts it:

"Within a year or two, saloons and houses of ill fame sprung up around the village (Fayette) much to the consternation of the law abiding citizens and 8 or 10 justices of the peace who had been sworn into office. All the good people were determined to put a stop to all of the lawlessness that accompanied the arrival of 'dens of evil.' Many workers with wives and children were squandering their hard-earned cash on liquor, women, and song and the numbers of men getting 'rolled' for their money increased.

"No saloon was permitted in town other than the bar which was maintained in the hotel. However after a loyal worker, Fred Hinks, (known as 'Pig Iron' Fred), became disabled in a plant accident, was allowed to open a tavern about a mile from the village on the Garden Road.

"The final spark that roused the citizens to arms occurred in August of 1880, when a girl escaped from the 'stockade' of a saloon and house operated by a man named Jim Summers. The place was located south of town and was surrounded by a high wooden fence to keep the curious from peering in and to keep the girls from leaving without permission, which was seldom given because many of the girls did not arrive of their own free will.

"One day in August a girl did escape and made her way to Fayette after two days wandering through the woods. The frightened girl found her way to the home of the deputy sheriff, assuming that he would protect her from her pursuers. Instead of affording her protection, he turned her over again to Summers, who by that time was waiting outside with a buggy. When the citizens discovered that they could not depend on their officers, a public meeting was called and it was decided to rescue the girl. Other bullies from the Summer's Gang were whooping it up in the saloon operated by 'Pig Iron' Fred about a mile east of town.

"The vigilante mob made its way to Pig Iron's and in a short time disposed of the Summer's Gang there with mops, sticks, clubs and any weapon at their disposal. They then proceeded to Summer's Stockade, rescued the girls from their 'jail' and put the torch to all the buildings. Within a few hours all that remained of the infamous resort were piles of smoking ashes. Summers, too, was apprehended in the unexpected raid. He was badly beaten and his clothes torn to shreds. The vigilantes left him bleeding and battered on the beach to die. The following morning some of his friends returned with the intention of giving him a decent burial, but his body had disappeared."

The recounting above seems very similar to what Osborn has been describing. These "stockades" were a plague on the region. In another side account dealing with Sac Bay, also known early on as Burnt Bluff Point is a small entry from R.L. Dodge:

"There is a legend about the town (later called Sac Bay) regarding a Frenchman who ran a saloon and bawdy house here in the 1870s. Workers at the Jackson Iron Co. furnaces were paid each month in gold pieces and saloons were barred from the town of Fayette. Workers took the narrow gauge railroad south to Sac bay and other saloons along the route to spend their money. During the purge of Fayette by a group of vigilantes it is said that the Frenchman at Sac Bay also became one of their victims. He escaped the mob by rowing a boat across the bay to Escanaba after burying his money, which was all gold coins, beneath a large beech tree. His despised place of business was burned to the ground. From there the story became embellished with each telling until it isn't known what became of the buried gold. Some say the man returned later and dug it up, others tell the story of the dying man drawing a map, which fell into other hands."

Both of the previous accounts back up Osborn's account. The look and feel of the activities near Fayette seem almost like déjà vu. Though not much is written on this subject, it's almost like any reference to these slave camps was either wiped away or forgotten. But if one digs deep enough, those dark, lost histories slowly come to light.

Manistique Pioneer Newspaper and Major Clarke

Another incident mentioned by Osborn is an attack on the *Schoolcraft County Pioneer* newspaper (still publishing today as the *Manistique Pioneer Tribune.*) and an assassination attempt on its editor, Major Clarke.

Wright E. Clarke was a newspaper man who arrived in Manistique in 1880. He was a veteran of the Civil War and had spent his life working in newspapers. He started Manistique's first newspaper, the *Schoolcraft County Pioneer*. His real name was Seymour Montgomery and he was on the run from a family he had deserted in Indiana. He never admitted his past even when his son showed up at his office. The two agreed to not speak of the relationship and his son, William Montgomery stayed in Manistique for many years.

In the *Schoolcraft County Pioneer*, Major Clarke began a campaign of temperance against local saloons and prostitution. The Chicago Lumbering Company had bought up most of the property in Manistique and had prohibited saloons, bawdy houses and drinking from all of their properties. If you purchased a piece of their property, " All lands shall never be used by the party of the second part for the business of manufacturing, storing, or selling intoxicating liquors, whether distilled or fermented, nor for a house or place of prostitution or assignation." was written into the deed. But, through a loophole and a vacant piece of property the lumbering company had missed, a man named Dan Heffron, along with his brother Dennis, was able to buy a piece outside of town along the Indian River and an unregulated piece of property in Manistique, thus erecting a place known as the Arcade Saloon. There was also a third brother named Larry who managed to remain in the background.

· DAN HEFFRON.

It was Heffron's places that Clarke was actively fighting against in his paper. Dan Heffron began operating his saloon and whorehouse with impunity. Though most in the community seemed against such an establishment, secretly many were patrons and the Heffron's business thrived.

In March 1883, Dan Heffron was charged for selling liquors without filing the proper paperwork. Heffron demanded a jury trial and got one. The case didn't go very far and Heffron found himself acquitted. This made him even bolder and in April on Election Day, Major Clarke was elected to be justice of the peace. It wasn't long and Dan and Dennis Heffron were both charged with having an open saloon on election day. Witnesses had people going in and out of the Arcade Saloon all day long.

A trial was held on May 2 1883, in which now Justice Clarke oversaw a jury trial. A unanimous conviction got the two brothers a 90 day jail sentence and a $25 fine. An appeal overturned the conviction.

Major Clarke was still running his newspaper and on May 7, 1883, a bullet came whizzing into the *Schoolcraft County Pioneer*'s office. Clarke tells about the shooting in his own words in his own newspaper on May 12, 1883.

> "Last Monday evening the editor of this paper attended a meeting of the Town Board, of which he is a member, and about 9 o'clock visited the Steamer *Messenger* which had just arrived; returning to his office engaged in writing. A little after 10 o'clock the office boy came in and soon left for his room. Just after he left the office some cold-blooded cowardly villain approached one of the west windows and fired a pistol, the ball coming through the window striking the table at which we sat, passing under the fingers of our left hand, just grazing two of them, striking the block of paper upon which we were writing,

threw the sheets up and over our right arm thus directing the ball upward where it struck the ceiling some ten feet from the floor.

"For a moment we were stunned, but recovering we looked toward the window and thought we saw the fiend in the act of shooting again. We jumped for the door and drew the only arm we carried, a very small revolver, opened the door, rushed to the corner of the building and saw in the darkness the form of a man about 20 feet distant. We fired and gave an outcry of alarm. The man increased the space between us; running in the direction of Rand Hall. Just then we heard another person trying to make their way around the west end of McAffee's shop and we advanced a few feet in that direction and fired a second shot; with what effect we know not. Thinking perhaps the would be murderers were better armed than we were, we retreated to our residence a short distance off. Sheriff McCanna was soon summoned and with him went back and looked over the ground but found that our unknown enemy had made good his escape. The shot was a very close one and evidently was intended for our head."

Major Clarke then goes on to explain why he feels he is a target:

"As to the cause of this midnight attempt to take our life we of course can only conjecture. It will be borne in mind that the editor of this newspaper has opposed the use of strong drinks. We have not only advocated temperance measures in our paper; but as one of the member of the township board, have strenuously opposed the approval of insufficient bonds. This has exasperated the advocates of rum to such an extent that for a number of weeks we have been the recipient of Ku Klux missives, warning us that if we valued our life it would be well to leave town; that our property was in danger of being destroyed, etc. These epistles were fictitiously signed and shoved under our office door. Having frequent acquaintance with such threatening letters during our editorial career we hardly gave them a thought; not believing we had a man in the county base enough to attempt the taking of life. But we were mistaken, and although the attempt has been made and providentially resulted in a failure, the animus of our enemy was sufficiently shown on Monday night."

Major Clarke expresses a grave naivete about the people of the area at the time, but in the ending of his editorial he alludes to a much bigger conspiracy at work here. "It's a prevalent thought that the deed was committed by men who had no interest in the questions at issue, but that they have done it for pay. Evidently, they were men who perhaps had no personal acquaintance with the writer. Men void of honor or manly courage. At this writing no clue to these midnight assassins has been obtained and are still at large. In this recital of the cowardly attempt upon our life we have given the facts with no attempt at sensationalism. If the time has come when men cannot express their honest convictions of right; if men are to be shot down in the dead hour of night for a conscientious adherence to principle, it is time and high time for honest people to ask 'Do our laws protect us as they should?' For us we will say that we have no love for the assassin's bullet; but the fear of it deters us not in the least when we have duty to perform."

He had now made himself a target. At the time it was rumored that the shooting had been done by Jim Summers or by one of his gang. Either he was hired by Dan Heffron or, since Sac Bay was in Schoolcraft County, he was also on Clarke's radar. Either way, Heffron would have been the first to be suspected in such an act. It would make sense to have someone else pull the trigger. It does display that these places had a connection with each other.

During this time, the Chicago Lumbering Company was doing an investigation of their own aimed at the "house of ill repute" that the Heffrons were running near the Indian River, near where M-94 crosses at present day. Some construction workers were hired by Dan Heffron to do some work on the bordello. They filed affidavits with the prosecuting attorney at the time, William Riggs. He in turn filed charges against all three brothers for "keeping a house of ill fame." Initially the brothers were found guilty, but on appeal they were acquitted. Seven of the witnesses against them disappeared the night before the trial.

In December 1883, the *Schoolcraft Pioneer*'s office was destroyed by arson. As Major Clarke mentions, he was getting these kinds of threats regularly. He admits he paid no heed to them and since the assassination didn't work, this was the next step. No one would be arrested or brought to trial over it. Later the next year, Major Clarke suffered from lead poisoning. He suffered from muscle weakness and was sent to Cleveland for hospitalization. His son ran the paper in his absence. The son went on to establish a rival paper in Manistique named the *Sun*.

The Heffrons seemed invincible with their continued legal victories. They operated unhindered and their logger's bordello thrived and expanded. In 1888, Dennis Heffron was elected Schoolcraft County Sheriff. Now they felt they could get away with anything. Even murder.

The Murder of Dan Dunn

This brings us to Dan Dunn. Dan Dunn's murder was big news when it happened. All of the local papers reported on it. It was perceived at the time to be a revenge killing, but the accusation that it was done on Mudge's orders adds a completely different perspective.

It all starts in the town of Seney. Known throughout the region as the wildest town in the north woods, Seney had a reputation for rough and dangerous living. The men who lived, worked and profited there were dubious and dangerous men. Dan Dunn was no different.

He came from Roscommon, where he had owned a saloon and a house of ill repute. Having continuous trouble with the law, he eventually hired someone to burn his place down so he could collect fire insurance on it. The local law didn't buy it and a warrant was issued for Dunn's arrest. He then went north and ended up in Seney. There he set up a small empire of vice. He opened a saloon and a bordello. He then constructed a stockade a few miles west of Seney, at Driggs River. He hired an individual named Mahoney to run the stockade, which was said to have vicious dogs that kept the inmates from escaping. A man named Dick Anger was the "Boss Pimp." Dan Dunn quickly became the controlling interest in most things in Seney. The woods were filled with loggers and business was good.

Enter the Harcourt brothers. There was six of them, Tom, Luke, Jim, Dick, Bill and Steve. Coming from Ireland, they were known for fighting at any provocation and they had a healthy dislike for Dan Dunn. They had been rivals with competing saloons back in Roscommon. Now they came to Seney, set up a saloon and hotel called the White House Hotel. They renewed their rivalry and there was nothing good-natured about it. Dunn didn't like anyone moving in on the sweet deal he had going for himself and the Harcourts were determined to get what Dunn had.

It says much that with six of them, they were cautious around Dan Dunn. Dunn was never without a gun at his side. He wore it at all times in his saloon. He was rumored to have killed at least two men at

Seney and buried them in the surrounding wilderness, because at different times they had sniffed around his Roscommon past. He put bullets in the back of both their heads. Dan Dunn was ruthless, yet those who encountered him said he could be quite personable. He dressed like a businessman rather than a saloon keeper. Dunn considered himself as the man about town in Seney and would even talk to newsmen of the day.

One such interview took place in June 1888. Dan Dunn was in his saloon playing billiards when a News Reporter approached him and tried to interview Dunn about his businesses, particularly the stockade. Dunn would never admit that it was his though everyone knew it was. It was the time where temperance movements were springing up and Seney was the capital of vice. A crusade against alcohol, gambling, and prostitution, including mentions of the stockades had been springing up in the newspapers and Seney was held up as an example on a regular basis. Headlines like "Seney's Dunn and Seney's Dens" which a Mrs. Obenauer had been preaching in her personal crusade against the stockades were adding pressure to "businessmen" like Dunn. She wrote, "Painted Women are kept locked in an outdoor stockade, where huge mastiffs are constantly on guard." What Dunn said to the reporter would not have helped much.

The reporter took Dunn's picture at the bar and Dunn reached around and took a picture down from the wall. It was a logging scene with loggers standing on a pile of logs. "Here take this. This is a bank scene we got taken. You see those fellows on the top row of logs? They are murderers. The chaps on the lower logs are only women assaulters. They don't work. They live upon somebody else. They are not in the habit of making a living. All those others in the picture, they kill women. We are all villains up here. We live on it. Take this picture along and show us up. Rogues gallery? Worse than rogues. Have old Governor Luce come out and size us up. He had a man sent here yesterday, before you got in, looking us up. He was over here at the telegraph office. The old governor told him to go to Iron Mountain. Follow him up and see what he does. Take a hand? No? Well, take a drink on me."

Dan Dunn's activities had become very public and it didn't bother Dunn in the least. He was bringing attention not only to the shady activities of Seney, but all across the north country. Publicity was not good for these kinds of endeavors. Word was getting out about Seney and none of it was good.

The Harcourts and Dunn were suspicious of each other. Each faction knew the other wanted them gone, preferably through Boot Hill. (Yes, Seney's Cemetery is called Boot Hill.) An argument that began during a card game resulted in events that would go down in U.P. legend.

Dan Dunn knew he was outnumbered by the Harcourts and at some point they would likely take advantage of it. He sent for an old friend named Jack Driscoll to come and work at his saloon as a bouncer. Unknown to Dunn, Driscoll had become friends with Luke Harcourt years earlier and they were cordial to each other, that is until a card game dispute caused Luke to accuse Driscoll of coming to work for Dunn just to get rid of the Harcourts. This was news to Driscoll who immediately got up and went to Dunn and then quit on the spot. He had no interest in coming between the two factions. Dunn was angry and threatened to shoot the next Harcourt he saw.

On June 25, 1891, Steve Harcourt went into Dan Dunn's saloon. He had been away camping upriver and was ready for a drink. He ordered drinks for himself and everyone in the saloon. Dunn declared that he wouldn't give a god-damned Harcourt a drink in his saloon. Harcourt started calling Dunn out for his lawlessness and the argument got hot quickly, so much so that Dunn broke a whiskey bottle over Steve Harcourt's head. He then pulled a gun and shot Steve through the jaw. Harcourt went for his gun, which was wrapped in a cloth and it hampered his shooting. His shot missed Dunn, hit the bar and ricocheted through a picture of John L. Sullivan behind the bar. Dunn shot again and hit Harcourt in the side and he staggered out of the door. His nephew found him bleeding in the street and took him home. His mother picked glass out of his head while the nephew ran for the doctor. It didn't help. In two days, Harcourt was dead.

Dunn was arrested for manslaughter. He was taken to Manistique and discharged after his preliminary hearing. The ruling was self-defense. Therefore, there were no reasons for charges. Dunn was free to go due to payment placed in the right hands to achieve such a verdict. Of course this didn't sit well with the Harcourts, who had sworn vengeance on Dunn but also stood to take over his very lucrative Seney businesses. Seney, being in Schoolcraft County, was under the jurisdiction of Manistique and the sheriff there, none other than Sheriff Dennis Heffron. Dunn swore out a complaint against the Harcourts. This sent the Sheriff to arrest the Harcourts in Seney.

Dunn, in the meantime, had gone to Trout Lake to see a friend, another saloon owner named Nevens. Trout Lake at the time was a track junction where the train from Seney ran to Trout Lake and then to Manistique or Sault Ste. Marie. The Harcourts had sworn vengeance on Dunn to the point of drawing straws to see who would pull the trigger. But then, they stood to gain considerably by killing Dan Dunn. Jim Harcourt drew the short straw.

Sheriff Heffron "arrested" the Harcourts. He took them into custody but never removed their weapons or handcuffed them. It seemed more like they were friendly neighbors. They boarded the train to Manistique for the Harcourts to answer the charges Dunn had filed against them. They had a stopover in Trout Lake. Heffron suggests they all go to Neven's saloon for a drink. The story goes that it was coincidence that Dunn and the Harcourts were in Trout Lake at the same time.

The stories vary a bit as to what actually happened as they often do, but the essentials are this. Dunn was staying with Nevens in an apartment above the saloon. Dunn came down the stairs with a gun stuck in the front of his pants into the main part of the saloon. He went over and was talking to Nevens at the bar.

Jim Harcourt tells the story like this:

> "After the acquittal of the murder of my brother in a justice's court, he swore out a warrant for me and my brothers, Dick and John. We were arrested and on our way from Seney to Manistique to be bound over to keep the peace, we had to stop at Trout Lake for a freight train. Together with Sheriff Heffron, we walked over to Jack Neven's saloon and had a drink. As we finished, Dan Dunn came downstairs with a revolver sticking out of his front pants' pocket. He ignored us and called all the rest up to have a drink. The sight of the man maddened me. He had a gun and had threatened to kill me on sight, and I knew when we met it must be Dunn's death or mine. I then shot five times at Dunn's back, every bullet hitting him, and he died without a word."

Jim Harcourt then stood over Dunn, put the empty gun to his head and pulled the trigger a few more times, all the while saying, "You killed my brother, now I've killed you. It's a horse apiece." Harcourt then turned and handed his gun to Sheriff Heffron. He said "I'm satisfied. I give myself up." Since the crime was committed in Trout

Lake, Heffron was obliged to turn Harcourt over to the Chippewa County Sheriff as they had crossed the county line on the train. Harcourt pleaded self-defense when his trial came up in Sault Ste. Marie.

Harcourt's story doesn't hold up. Some witnesses said that Harcourt came through the door and started shooting. At one point Harcourt professed he thought Dunn "made a movement toward his pocket and he feared for his life." Patrons at the bar said Dunn was reaching for a wallet to pay for drinks when Harcourt shot him. Shooting Dunn in the back as many times as he did implies that Dunn was taken completely by surprise. Dunn was shot in the back so closely by Harcourt that the fabric in Dunn's clothes ignited from the gunfire.

The fact that Sheriff Dennis Heffron did nothing when the threat arose, allowed all of the Harcourts to keep their guns and they weren't handcuffed, lends credence to Chase Osborn's claim that this was a hit and not a revenge killing. It also stands to reason that if they had not crossed the county line and the murder would have occurred in Schoolcraft County, the Harcourts would have gotten off as easily as Dunn had for shooting Steve Harcourt.

Consequently, the Chippewa County judge tried James Harcourt before a jury. He was sentenced to 10 years in prison at the Marquette Correctional Institute. He returned to Seney after his release, rejoining his family.

The Heffrons were eventually brought down. Dan Heffron was arrested, along with several of his prostitutes, in 1891. The arrest warrant was carried out when the sheriff, his brother Dennis, was away. In the process the State of Michigan Attorney General, Adolphus Ellis, was asked to step in when it was complained that the prosecuting attorney, William Riggs was reluctant to prosecute houses of ill repute. The Attorney General took the case from Riggs and suspended Sheriff Heffron's authority due to the obvious conflict of interest. Things were looking bad for Dan Heffron. The trial was held in February and March of 1892.

Dan Heffron knew of the likelihood of his conviction and made arrangements for an escape. He was free on bond so when the word got to him that the jury was coming back after an hour of deliberation, he decided to run. One of the local livery men hooked up a sleigh and ran by Dan Heffron who grabbed the sled, without it slowing down, jumped into it and covered up with buffalo robes. A pursuit was organized but he was not to be found. A $100 reward was offered, but

Dan Heffron disappeared. The result was the end of his reign of intimidation and terror. Though there is dispute whether his bordello was a stockade/prison or not, he was certainly tied into a much broader collective of owners of these types of places, an early loose cartel of prostitution and crime. It was well known that the women were often moved from one place to the next to provide "fresh" women for the loggers. The owners most certainly interacted with each other creating a network between not just the stockades, but the other bordellos that they were supplying. The girls were shipped in and out of towns on an organized vice circuit. To see just how organized they were, once again we return to Chase Osborn's account.

Osborn's account of the stockade's end in Florence, WI:

> "We called a meeting and organized the Citizen Regulators. The meeting was such a hummer and so many joined that the sheriff and District Attorney had a street duel the next day, growing out of a row that was caused by each trying to shift the blame upon the other. I had publicly charged them both with being controlled by the Mudge gang. The district Attorney shot the sheriff through the lungs. A lot of the sheriff's friends got a rope to hang the lawyer, who really was one of the worst of citizens, while the sheriff had told several that he intended to join the regulators.
>
> "I started to Madison and Milwaukee to enlist influence and see the governor, in order to have the district attorney removed and have a man appointed who would enforce the law. All the way to Milwaukee I was harassed by telegrams for my arrest. The gang tried to capture me at the train, but I learned of their plans in time to elude them. Then we had a wild race through the woods to the Michigan line. If they had caught me in Wisconsin they were going to finish me in some way.
>
> "The pursuit kept up almost to Iron Mountain, which was nearly as bad as Florence at the time. I dodged them but was afraid to stop at Iron Mountain because the local authorities there were believed to be under the control of the Mudge outlaws. It was night. I had expected to take an evening train. Prevented from doing this, I ran two miles through the woods to Commonwealth. There, one of my faithful printers, an Irish lad named Billy Doyle, had a team in waiting. Hastily climbing into the buckboard and taking the lines, I lashed the horses into a gallop. Over my shoulders I could see the gang coming

on foot, on horse and in rigs. I had a colt's revolver and could shoot it quite well enough. Billy had thrown in a Winchester. I made up my mind they would not take me in Wisconsin without a fight.

"On the outskirts of Iron Mountain I gave the reins to Billy and jumped out and went on alone. Safely making a detour of the town, I took the railroad track and hiked southward towards law and order. I was in Michigan. Between Keel Ridge and Quinnesec, three men stepped out of the gloom and leveled guns at my head. I obeyed their order to hold up my hands and they took me back to Iron Mountain by main force, and not a sign of a legal warrant. They were Mudge agents. It was after midnight. I made a big roar as soon as I got where anybody could hear. In spite of the racket I made they took me to a place which was not the jail and locked me in a room. Before they got me confined, I managed to send word to Cook and Flannigan, whose firm of attorneys at Norway (Michigan) was the ablest on the range. The late Hon. A. C. Cook got to me and secured my release. To this day I do not know how he did it.

"I continued on my way. Efforts were made to stop me at Marinette and Green Bay. These were unsuccessful. Finally I got to Milwaukee where I had a number of strong friends. Lemuel Ellsworth had just become chief of police, and the present Milwaukee chief, John T. Janssen, was on the detective staff. I went to the central station to call upon them, as they were old friends of mine during my police reporter days. The chief handed me a telegram to read. It was for my arrest. They had sent it to the wrong place. I told my story. The Chief said, 'Glad to see you, Chase. Now let's do something about these hell-hounds. I will wire I have you and ask them to send for you with a strong guard. This will possibly bring a crowd of them down, and I will throw them all into the bullpen.

"During the afternoon I received a telegram signed 'H.P. Cory.' It read 'Don't come back. They are going to kill you if you do.' I knew it as a fake at once, for the preacher would have had me come back and be killed rather than have me run away from the fine fight I had started.

"I saw rugged Jeremiah M. Rusk, then governor of Wisconsin, and secured the appointment of a clean lawyer named Howard E. Thompson as District Attorney to succeed the Mudge gang lawyer. Governor Rusk gave me every encouragement. "Go after them, boy," he said, "and if you need help just say the word. I'll back you with the troops if it is necessary.

"I made my way back north about as rapidly as I had fled. The gang was in a panic when they saw me and heard the support of the governor had fortified me with. I had it told to them in as amplified and impressive a manner as possible and then I played it up in my paper with all my might and type. The gang was on the run from that time, but it was not beaten yet. Claudius B. Grant was a circuit judge in the adjacent region of Michigan. He became a terror to the bad men and women and clearly showed what a man rightly constituted can do with the law in his own hands. He was waging a solitary war against the gang and sheriffs and prosecuting attorneys who were their tools. Finally he made it so hot for them on his side, and we so reciprocated on our side that the bad people began to look for other and less troublesome pastures. They fled to Seney, Trout Lake, Ewen, Sidnaw, Hurley and other points in the Lake Superior country out of Grant's jurisdiction, and out of our reach, where they operated for some years without molestation. There was a temporary revival of outlawry in Judge Grant's district because the gang had gotten rid of him by designedly electing him to the Supreme Court of Michigan.

"Shootings occurred by day and night, and the fight was a real battle. At first the gang had nearly all the law officers on its side. By degrees we changed this. The average fellow in office is quick to try to pick the winning side. These trimmers, usually so despicable, were a real help to us because they trimmed gradually to our side.

"Mudge withdrew his worst operations to more remote spots in the woods. The regulators determined to clean all of them out. The law was too slow under the conditions that existed and the punishments inadequate. At the time there was really no law against white slavery and procuring.

"Pat McHugh, a bully and retired prize fighter, was Mudge's head man. Nearly everybody was afraid of him. He had even been to fight in the daytime with his backers at hand,

and he was fairly quick with a gun, but could not fan. On a day agreed upon the Regulators, armed with Winchester rifles, Colt revolvers, and blacksnake whips, started on a rodeo. They drove the toughs off the street. Those who did not move quickly enough were lashed smartly with the blacksnakes. Theirs had been a reign of terror long enough. It was our turn. They showed as many temperaments as one could find among any men and women. Some were whimpering cowards. Others were sullen.

"The women were most bold and loudest in profanity and vulgarity. McHugh was one of the first to run. He hid in the swamp stockade with half a dozen others of the gang. The regulators rode down against them. They opened a hot fire with the Winchester repeaters. The Regulators replied and charged. It fell to Bill Noyes to capture Pat McHugh. The bully had often boasted what he would do to Bill if he ever got a chance. Now he fled into the swamp, revolver in hand. Bill saw him and ran after him. They dodged from tree to tree, Indian fashion, exchanging shots from time to time. Bill was too good of a woodsman for McHugh. He loaded his gun as he ran and soon had the drop on the leader of the outfit. McHugh fell on his knees and pleaded for mercy. Bill spared him. He said to me only a short time ago, 'Chase I reckon I oughta killed that red-headed devil that day I got him in the swamp, but I'm kinda glad I didn't, 'cause it goes agin the grain with me to kill anything I can't eat.'

"After that we burned a number of stockades and soon had the community so fit to live in that I spent four happy years there. What became of Mudge will never be told. Only a half-dozen Regulators ever knew."

Chase Osborn's account of the stockades saves their existence from oblivion. The reality of the stockades would have faded into the past, forgotten, lost to time. This women's slavery ring infested the north country and is an early gang of organized crime. The number of identified stockades indicates that there were likely several more that weren't.

Postscript: Lottie Morgan

I wanted to include this story as a sidebar to what has been written previously. It is about a well-known prostitute who has become legend in the western end of the Peninsula. This took place in Ironwood/ Hurley, twin cities divided only by the Montreal River, which is the Michigan/Wisconsin state line. Hurley was known as "Hell on Earth" while Ironwood was the moral side of the tracks. Hurley's reputation made Seney's sound like amateur hour. Silver Street, which was six blocks long, Hurley's main street, contained nothing but vice. There were 63 saloons in those six blocks! All had available prostitutes, liquor and gambling. Of course, Hurley is one of the places mentioned in Osborn's narrative.

This brings us to Lottie Morgan. She was also known as Lotta. Her real name was Laura Whittlesay. As a young girl she was captured and placed in a stockade. It had a high wooden fence and it was said that escape was impossible unless a girl was purchased by a patron who happened to fall in love with an inmate. This stockade was described in *Call It North Country,* like this, "A log pen with a single entrance guarded by savage dogs. Inside the pen was a house consisting of a single large room, its floor covered with close-spaced pallets, or workbenches. Here a dozen girls labored, and the dogs were trained to prevent them from escaping, but not to prevent the customers from entering." Lottie Morgan escaped. She went over the wall and broke her leg as she dropped to the ground. She then hobbled and crawled a half mile through the snow. When she was found, it raised such an outcry that the stockade was burned to the ground that night.

Lottie then tried to disappear for a couple of years, even attempting to enter a convent, but they wouldn't have her, essentially driving her back out onto the streets. Lottie was a fallen woman, irredeemable to many.

She went to work in Hurley in the saloons, singing and performing onstage. Her popularity with the locals was high and she never starved for attention. She was loved by the men of all classes, even those who came over in the night for clandestine debauchery from Ironwood. The local ladies didn't care for her at all.

By all reports, she thoroughly loved the nightlife of Hurley. Lottie would open and close the saloons, all the while being the life of the party. Men often stated that they were in love with her.

In 1890 it all came to an end. Lottie was leaving John Sullivan's saloon. She was walking down an alley to where her rooms were and an axe hit her in the face. Another blow was struck to her head and she was stabbed with a knife. Lottie Morgan was dead. It was April 11, 1890. She was twenty-seven years old.

Fig. 9-3: Lottie Morgan as she appeared in Hurley during her saloon days.

Fig. 9-4: A portrait of the ill-fated Lottie Morgan. Probably taken not long before her murder.

A passerby found the body in the early morning. At first he thought she was drunk and then quickly realized she was dead. The ax was found leaning in a woodshed near where Lottie lay. Blood and hair was stuck to it. A gun was found in her purse, but it had never fired. She was taken by complete surprise. She still had all of her jewelry and there was $20 in her purse so this wasn't about robbery.

A cry went out from many of the citizens, mostly men, for the killer to be found but it seemed to fall on deaf ears. The police seemed to be doing something, but mostly they speculated instead of investigating. Lottie's position in life seemed to prevent a serious investigation. The newspapers at the time touted her death as a fine example of everything that was wrong with Hurley. The sheriff commented that it was a Jack the Ripper-like murder. The Oshkosh Northwestern newspaper interpreted it like this "Lottie Morgan, who was about twenty-seven years old and belonged to the demi monde, was found murdered behind a saloon in Hurley this morning. Her head was split open, cut off and awfully mutilated with an axe. The police are working on a clue. This is a Jack the Ripper case." The Ripper murders had occurred only two years previous and since no one was ever caught, speculation ran rampant at the time that Jack the Ripper had escaped to America and dozens of murders were being blamed on him.

One of the other rumors that went around at the time was that she had either overheard plans for or witnessed a bank robbery. The story varies as to which it was. It was one of the local theories at the time as to a motive.

One of the largest funerals ever held in Hurley was Lottie's. It was held in the town opera house and was attended by many from all around. One of the papers, the *Oshkosh Northwestern,* wrote this:

> "The funeral of the late Lotta Morgan took place here yesterday afternoon. Her remains had lain in state in the Hurley Opera House for four days and were viewed by thousands of people. The elite of the town together with the ministers of the gospel assembled together with the citizens and the disreputable characters and mourned the untimely taking of a fallen woman—a woman who had fallen to the lowest depths of degradation."

The murder was never solved and many believe it was because the police didn't care enough about a woman of her social status.

Whatever the reason, Lottie's death remains a mystery to this day. Was it a senseless killing? Maybe not. When Lottie escaped from the stockade causing it to be consequently burned down because of her, she most certainly made some very powerful enemies. It could also explain why she sought sanctuary in a convent. It would also explain her name change as her only alternative was to work in the saloons. Since the stockade gangs often employed assassins, this seems very possible to me and it explains a lot about the murder. The rumor of her involvement with a bank robbery was probably a tale of misdirection at the time. It is a case that cries out for justice to this day.

Author's note: It is well known in the Ironwood/Hurley area that Lottie's ghost haunts a place called Dawn's Never Inn. The tavern is situated where Lottie was killed and there are dozens of stories of her apparition appearing. The Inn was featured on the TV series "America's Most Terrifying Places."

There is no doubt that over the years there has been a conspiracy of cover-up perpetrated by communities and historians to wipe away the subject of the stockades. They almost succeeded. The idea of slave camps dotting the landscape of the U.P. is and should be abhorrent on every level, but it is also a part of the history and sometimes dark heritage that prevailed for so many years without consequence. As Osborn states, technically this wasn't illegal at the time. It was rampant and was prevalent throughout the Upper Peninsula and Northern Wisconsin.

10   The Artwork of the Shamans

Fig. 10-1: Agawa Rock where the Native American pictographs are painted.

The war was on and it was time to make a stand. The tribes of the Iroquois had expanded too far. They had all of the lands toward the rising sun, now their greed seemed to drive them toward the Great Lakes, particularly Gitchee Gummee. No more. As Myeengun stood at the sacred rock, he knew his power was great enough to stop the intruders. The tribes of the Ojibwa would win. He had foreseen the battle. He called upon the power of the Michepezhoo, the beast of copper that lived below the surface of Gitchee Gumee. Myeengun caused the lake to rise against the Iroquois. The Michepezhoo rose up and consumed the Iroquois. They all drowned. Myeengun went to the sacred rock and alongside the pictures of his ancestors, he painted his own. He told of the battle and their victory. He left it there on the sacred rock for all generations to know; this was the land of the Ojibwa, respect it or die.

This is one of the tales that the dozens of paintings on the Agawa Rock depict. These "pictographs" have been left at Agawa Rock over a period of centuries by Ojibwa shamans when the entire Lake Superior basin was looked at as one territory.

They were first described to Henry Rowe Schoolcraft by a local Ojibwa shaman named Shingwauk (Little Pine) when he worked as an Indian Agent in Sault Ste. Marie, Michigan. He recorded them in his book *Intellectual Capacity and Character of the Indian Race* (1851). Though he never saw them, their locations were described, 100 miles north of the Soo along the Lake Superior shore. In 1958, Selwyn Dewdney reported them on the side of a cliff.

The area is now known as Lake Superior Provincial Park in Canada, between the Montreal River and the town of Wawa. Agawa Rock is one of the attractions of the park, drawing thousands annually.

Though archaeologists are unable to identify the artists of most of the drawings, two names have been attached to some: Myeengun and Shingwaukonce. Both are shamans from Michigan's Upper Peninsula. Their drawings, as well as those unidentified, have become images known all around the Lake Superior basin and are frequently used as icons of the area.

Agawa Rock's importance culturally, spiritually and archaeologically can't be overemphasized. Ojibwa pictographs are found all around the Lake Superior Basin, but nowhere are there so many of them in one place. Nor are any so artistically developed and give so many glimpses into native beliefs and legends. They also describe events of historical record in an oral culture.

Shingwauk told Schoolcraft about a chief named Myeengun (Wolf of the Mermaid) who lived on the banks of the Carp River in the eastern Upper Peninsula. Their territory was the Straits of Mackinac, part of Lake Huron, north to the Soo. He was considered the Chief of the Ojibwa throughout the area. His name appears on a treaty in Ottawa, Canada. Myeengun was skilled in the rituals of the Meda, or Grand Medicine Lodge, the society of Ojibwa shamans. Myeengun's influence was great and he led a war party in canoes up the Carp River, through Trout Lake, down the Tahquamenon and into Whitefish Bay. Then they paddled across Lake Superior, where they joined forces with the Agawa band of Ojibwa to do battle with the Iroquois. Through magic, the Iroquois were drowned. To commemorate the event, Myeengun left pictograph paintings at Agawa and somewhere along the Carp River, but those have never been found.

Some of the pictographs represent this event with canoe figures that have animal images alongside depicting their clans: thunderbird, beaver, and crane. These were left as a warning to others who might invade the land of the Ojibwa.

Symbols of magical protectors such as the Michipezhoo, and Mikinok, the land tortoise, have become well known images from around the Lake Superior area. The most often seen grouping of pictographs is that of the Michepezhoo cluster. There may have been more to this group, but a large chip of rock shaved off above the Michipezhoo and fell into Lake Superior.

The author of these drawings has been known right along. Shingwaukonce (Little White Pine) was from the Grand Island tribe, in Munising Bay, also on Lake Superior. He became Grand Shaman of the Lake Superior Ojibwa. According to oral histories, he went to Agawa to gather fresh power on a vision quest. He called forth Michipezhoo, the guardian spirit of the underworld and minerals, especially copper. Shingwaukonce completed his fast, finished rituals which included drawing the rock art, and then led his warriors in a revolt against prehistoric copper miners.

There are many small individual rock art drawings. Some are very clear and easy to identify, while others are identifiable by slight ochre color changes in the rocks. Many of the pictographs have faded, and worn away. Nonetheless they are breathtaking. It's like looking back through time, each drawing being different stops on a time travel trip. The artists of these are unknown and probably always will be.

All of the pictographs are painted in a red ochre mined from an island a few miles north of Agawa Europeans have called Devil's Warehouse Island. The ochre was mixed with fish oil and animal grease, then dabbed on the cliffs. They are remarkably durable and have withstood the vicious elements of Lake Superior. The reason that they have lasted this long is because the rock secretes and clear mineral fluid that acts as a natural varnish. There are reports from Ojibwa natives that a huge slab of some of the best paintings fell into the water several years ago.

Another major cluster of pictographs is called the horse and rider group. This was also painted by Shingwaukonce after a ten-day fast

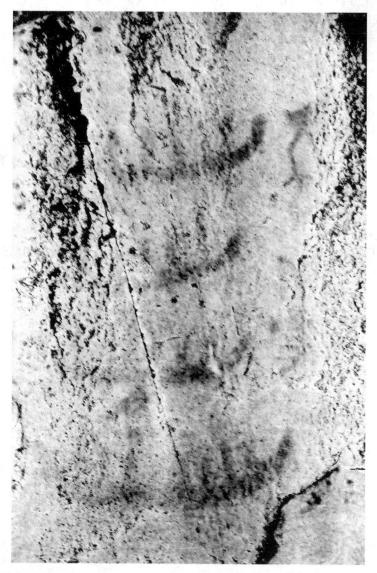

Fig. 10-2a: Myeengun's war party. The canoes and the clan symbols can be seen on the rock.

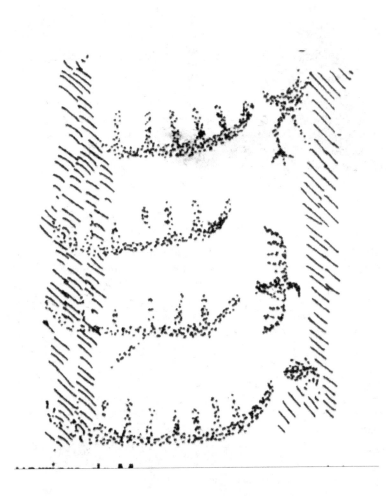

Fig. 10-2b: An interpretation drawing of the war party panel

Fig. 10-3a: Michiphezu panel. The spirit of Lake Superior, the great copper beast that lives beneath the waters is pictured in the top right.

Fig. 10-3b: An interpretation of the Michepezu panel with the surrounding drawings.

associated with a ritual duel between Shingwaukonce and a rival shaman over the spiritual leadership of the Lake Superior Ojibwa. The drawings represent Shingwaukonce's power, like a primitive resume, and they describe his shamanic abilities.

A cross appears in the group. This represents a fourth-degree shaman and predates Christianity. The four spheres depict prayer circles. There is a faint louse in front of the horse which according to legend represents a time when Shingwaukonce turned himself into a louse so that he could ride a raven into the spirit world. The horse and rider is Shingwaukonce himself.

The pictographs are extremely delicate and should never be touched. They are looked on as religious objects by the Ojibwa, and it is not unusual to find offerings of tobacco and sweetgrass left at Agawa Rock.

Besides Agawa Rock, there are several other pictograph sites in Lake Superior Provincial Park. Some have been located in the Pukaskwa (Puckasaw) area of Ontario; also at Schreiber, Ontario, which has been kept undisclosed to protect the pictographs. Nipigon Bay, Ontario has many similar to Agawa Rock. There is also a small rock art site on a small island near Marquette, Michigan.

The rock art is a prehistoric heritage left behind for all who live around the Lake Superior basin. They represent a time shrouded in mystery, and a culture that was nearly lost. They were created as a way of communicating across time and into the spirit worlds. In a book called *Spirits On Stone*, the pictographs are summed up best this way: "The pictograph site location can energize or calm us. The setting certainly leads us away from the 20th century into a more natural world. In some ways, a poet can get closer to the site than a scientist."

Author's note: Information for this article came for a book called *Spirits on Stone* by Thor and Julie Conway, published by Heritage Discoveries Publications, San Luis Obispo, California. Other information came from *Agawa Rock Indian Pictographs* by the Ontario Ministry of Natural Resources.

11 The Sinking of the *South Shore*

Fig. 11-1: The ship the South Shore as it appeared before the shipwreck.

In 1909, a captain from Grand Marais by the name of Ora Endress purchased a small wooden steamer called the *South Shore*. With the railroad gone from Grand Marais, a vital link had been taken away from those who remained in the community. Something had to be done to fill that void. Endress's idea was to make regular supply runs along the south shore of Lake Superior from Whitefish Bay to Marquette. The upper deck of the ship held cabins, allowing Endress to book passengers as well. He scheduled the *South Shore* to make stops at places like Whitefish Point, Vermillion, the Two-Hearted River, Grand Marais and Au Sable Point. The *South Shore* was a regular sight on the lake and an occasional visitor to Au Sable Point Lighthouse, dropping off supplies or personnel for the light station.

Endress did quite well with his business until late November 1912. November is never a good time to have to sail the Great Lakes. The unpredictability and the utter and complete violence of the gales have taken hundreds of ships to the bottom. And hurricane-force winds and blizzards can—and often do—come with these November storms. Endress was sailing the *South Shore* toward Grand Marais from Sault Ste. Marie when the ship became engulfed in blinding snow. A northeast gale had blown up, and things were getting dicey fast. The waves had built, and it became apparent that the *South Shore* wouldn't be able to get into Grand Marais harbor.

Endress had spent many years on the Great Lakes. He was well seasoned and knowledgeable, but now he had to make a difficult decision. With four passengers and ten crewmen on the ship, he chose the option he thought would give the ship and those on board their best chances of survival. He decided to try to ride out the storm in the open water. He put the bow to the wind and hoped for the best.

The storm blew mercilessly into the night. But Endress, keeping his bow to the waves, was working his way northeast out into Lake Superior. He had sailed almost halfway to Caribou Island, about twenty-five miles out from Grand Marais. The waves were beating against the ship and rolling over the decks. Slowly, the ship's seams started to open. A huge wave came and swept away the part of the cabin house. Another wave pounded in part of the wheelhouse. The raging surf broke out windows and covered the *South Shore* in a sheet of ice. Water coming in the hull reached the boiler fires and extinguished them. The *South Shore* was without power.

The helpless ship was driven before the storm. It rose and fell between the massive troughs of waves. The wet and cold passengers and crew all manned the hand pumps, trying to keep the beleaguered ship afloat. It was a long night, but as morning rolled around, the ship was still afloat.

In the morning, the Grand Marais Life Saving Station spotted the *South Shore* about ten miles out. Endress, who was likely too busy trying to save his ship, wasn't flying any distress flags. But Captain Trudell, Commander of the Grand Marais Life Savers, deduced that they might need help, and there just might have been a small desire to take out the station's new motor-powered surfboat, named the *Audacity*. The days of rowing were behind the lifesavers—at least as long as the motor didn't conk out. Motorized surfboats made the Life-Saving Service more efficient. They were quicker to respond to wrecks and quicker to unload passengers and crew. It had been a major improvement for the lifesavers and those who depended on them.

When they reached the *South Shore*, the ship was nearly awash and foundering, as it was very full of water. They tried everything. They

Fig. 11-1: The South Shore after it wrecked. Grand Sable sand dunes can be seen in the background. The captain is standing on the top of the boat which remained above water for a while until Lake Superior broke it apart.

jettisoned the cargo and helped work the pumps. At one point, they even tried to rebuild the boiler fire, but it was to no avail. A decision had to be made. The lifesavers took off the four passengers and the ten crewmen and headed back to shore.

The abandoned *South Shore* was now at the mercy of Lake Superior. It was blown west toward Au Sable Point and Grand Sable Dunes. All the while, Lake Superior continued to batter the ship. Eventually, it rolled toward the shore and sank in twelve feet of water. where Au Sable Point meets Grand Sable Dunes, west of the Devil's Log Slide.

The loss of the *South Shore* caused considerable hardship, since it was carrying the winter supplies for many along the route. The winter was lean for those waiting for the *South Shore* to make its run, a run it never completed.

The *South Shore* can sometimes still be seen. It's quite visible when standing atop the log slide and gazing across the vastness of Au Sable Point, with the lighthouse in the distance. When you look down at Lake Superior, look below the log slide but toward Au Sable. The shape of the *South Shore* can be seen under the shallow water. From time to time, the sand will cover and uncover the remains of the ship. So, like the ghost it is, the *South Shore* appears only occasionally, when the conditions are just right.

~ ~ ~

Author's Note: I came across this story while researching my book, *Au Sable Point Lighthouse, Beacon on Lake Superior's Shipwreck Coast.* I found the photos too late to make it into the book, while the story is a part of the finished edition along with dozens of other stories like this. If you enjoyed this tale of life on Lake Superior, please consider picking up a copy of my book. It can be ordered through my website www.mikelclassen.com or through any bookstore, just ask.

12 Who was Mother Ontonagon?

This is a picture I recently came across (see next page). The back of the card reads: "Mother Ontonagon, 120 Years Old." I suspect it is highly unlikely that she is actually this old but the accompanying information is fascinating just the same:

"Mother Ontonagon, original photograph owned by C.E. Haring. Ontonagon is an Indian name in the Chippewa dialect meaning 'my bowl is gone.' In the primitive days of the region, a little Indian girl of the Chippewa Nation came to the edge of the river where it empties into Lake Superior, with her little wooden bowl to get a drink and while dallying with it in the water it slipped from her hand and glided off upon the moving surface beyond her reach when she, in a moment of excitement and sorrow she exclaimed 'On-to-na-gon,' *Oh, my bowl is gone.*

"From the incident, the name of Ontonagon was given by Chippewa Indians to the river, which stole away the bowl of their bright-eyed little girl into Lake Superior, and subsequently the same name was given to the village and the county. The little maid referred to was afterward known as Mother Ontonagon. A version of the picture above was hung in the Ontonagon School for many years.

"It is said that she always carried a skunk skin, so as to be immune from smallpox. She was a well-known native throughout the county and lived to a ripe old age."
Escanaba Daily Press, December 29, 1871.

Armed with my copy of the picture of Mother Ontonagon, I took a trip to the Ontonagon Historical Society Museum located in downtown Ontonagon. The photo had piqued my interest enough that I really wanted to find out who this was.

Fig. 12-1: The portrait of Mother Ontonagon, "120 years" that inspired my search for the story behind the picture.

As far back as when Alexander Henry in 1766 adventured into the region and was shown the Ontonagon Boulder, a vast mass of float copper that the Natives worshipped (already discussed), the region was long known as Ontonagon. With photography not becoming prevalent until approximately 1850, it seemed very unlikely that the person in the picture was the same as the Mother Ontonagon of legend even if she had lived to be 120 years old. I wanted to find out who she really was.

I tucked away the picture in a protective case and headed for Ontonagon country. I was hoping that the Ontonagon Historical Society Museum would have enough information that I might be able to put the real name to the face and maybe even learn something about her. I knew it was a long shot. This would have been during a time when anything Native American was considered unimportant and/or expendable. A record of her real identity was likely lost forever. My hopes were not high.

When I got there, I pulled out my copy of the picture and asked the attendant if there was any information on her. She smiled and said "Twice this summer we've had someone come in and say they were related to her and were looking for information on her. They were researching genealogy and she was one of their ancestors. They confirmed from the picture she was who they were looking for."

What luck! Or maybe it was more than luck and she just needed to come out into the light. The attendant took me to a file cabinet and pulled out a folder labeled "Mother Ontonagon." It was thin, very thin, but at least it was something.

Her name was Go-Da-Quay. She was a local Native American born around 1781 near La Pointe, Wisconsin. There is some dispute to her age but this is within a year. At some point she married an Andrew Godfree. The spelling of the name varies between Godfree and Godfrey. She became known as Charlot or Charlotte. Both spellings are in the records.

Her husband, Andrew, was a trapper. At 70 years old she claimed to remember the battle of Seven Oaks in 1816 between the Hudson's Bay Company and the Northwest Fur Company in Minnesota. Twenty-two people were killed. She would have been around thirty-five at this time.

Ontonagon was the site of a long-established Native American village. The Ontonagon River was a source of fish and the surrounding hills gave them copper. They traded with the trappers and other tribes. Go-Da-Quay learned these things well.

She had five children. One was Louis Godfrey, who died in Ontonagon at the age of 70. He preceded his mother in death by two weeks. She taught the traditions and stories she had learned to her children and grandchildren.

She was considered a fixture around Ontonagon. Her obituary called her one of "Ontonagon's ancient landmarks." When the first permanent settlers came in the 1840s, Go-Da-Quay would have been around 60 years old. Over the years it is likely (no proof of this) that her advancing age earned her the nickname of "Mother Ontonagon."

She died at the age of 106 to 108. Most sources say 108, but since there is no actual birthdate, it is somewhere thereabouts. In her obituary it says that "she was probably the oldest member of the Chippewa tribe on Lake Superior." It was March 24th, 1889.

I closed the file, smiled and put the folder back in the file cabinet. The woman who had helped me earlier had left me to myself while I looked for information. I walked out to the door and said thanks. "Any luck?" she asked.

"Yes, I found what I was looking for," I replied.

"Good, well, come back again."

"I'm sure I will." I knew it would only be until the next project. There's always a next project.

Fig. 13-1: The old Christmas sign. It was removed a couple of years ago. I kind of miss it.

Christmas belongs to the Upper Peninsula. It's all ours. Not the holiday... *the town*, Christmas, Michigan. It's been ours for eighty years and it always will be. Christmas (the town) is where Christmas (the holiday) is on display all year 'round and all the trappings of the season are never taken down, because, in Christmas (the town), Christmas (the holiday), brings visitors all year to investigate the place that is named for the most celebrated holiday in the world.

If one were setting out to name a town after this particular holiday, there is no better location for it. Christmas looks the part, not only from a man-made aspect, but from a geographical standpoint as well.

Upon entering Christmas, especially during the winter, it looks like a vision of the North Pole. Christmas is three miles west of Munising in

Fig. 13-2: Christmas Mall and post office where everyone goes for the "Christmas" stamp.

the middle of a snow belt. Since it is also on the Lake Superior shoreline, winter weather conditions can get very severe. Although it isn't really the North Pole, it certainly could be an outpost.

In the center of town there are reproductions of Santa and Mrs. Claus with a large North Pole post beside them. Businesses reflect the spirit of the community's name and follow along with the theme, such as Mrs. Klaus' cabins and Foggy's Bar that features the "Reindeer Room".

Christmas is a quiet place but there is still plenty to do. There is a cross-country ski trail and snowmobile trail for winter activities as well as two nightspots and a casino. Several motels and resorts offer cabins for visitors. In the warmer seasons, there is everything to do that can be found in a lakeshore town including a nice park, and Bay Furnace campgrounds. A newer business is the Paddler's Village, a camping/yurt experience on Lake Superior for paddlers. Tourism is a staple income for the area and Christmas is no exception. It is an excellent destination point with a novel theme.

Before Christmas was Christmas, there was a fur trade fort erected near what would become Bay Furnace on Grand Island bay. It was

Fig. 13-3: The Bay Furnace at Christmas before it was restored. This sits near where Fort Thompson once stood.

owned by the Northwest Fur Trade Company, which was in competition with the Hudson's Bay Company for furs from Native Americans. It was named Fort Thompson, after David Thompson, a surveyor and mapmaker for the Northwest Fur Company, and was built in 1763. It is believed that the agent who worked the fort was the first European to settle in the area. Very little is known about the fort but it stayed in operation until 1820, when the Northwest Fur Company went bankrupt.

After that, it was known as the Bay Furnace and the land surrounding it became the town of Onota. Beginning in 1869, there were immense furnace structures along the shore of Lake Superior, where they smelted iron from the Ishpeming iron range. A 1400-foot-long dock provided mooring for the ships transporting the smelted iron. Over 50 kilns were in operation at Bay Furnace's peak. Thousands of tons of pig iron were smelted in these furnaces.

In 1870, the town received a post office, designated "Onota." The population reached a peak 500 in 1877. During that summer, a dry spell made the surrounding woods volatile. A fire began that burned for several days and at one point swept down on Onota, destroying it and all of the kilns. It was the end of Onota, or so it seemed. The name was moved 15 miles to the west to Onota township. Bay Furnace remained all but forgotten. The Bay Furnace company had been going bankrupt before the fire and the demise of the Bay Furnace operations seems to have been a blessing in disguise.

Christmas (the town) came into being a little over eighty years ago in 1939, when a local individual decided to start a Christmas-product-oriented factory and call it "Christmas Industries." Julius Thorson, a retired state conservation officer, bought the land and had the property registered under his business name of Christmas at the Alger County Records Office. The section always appeared in the plat books under the name of "Christmas," so the area simply retained the name.

The industry was short-lived, and burned down the next year and was never rebuilt, but the name stayed on the plat maps, and stuck with the small community. Thorson had originally planned to establish an elaborate tourist complex on the land he had purchased, but the factory was the only part of the plan that materialized.

At the same time, a beaver farmer named Walter Giedrojc had a profitable farming venture going on. During prohibition, he augmented his furry occupation by bootlegging bathtub booze on the side, selling it out of the back door of his home. When prohibition ended, he went legitimate and converted his home into a tavern named "Beaver Park." The building still functions as a tavern (and restaurant) now known as Foggy's.

Development of Christmas (the town) as a resort area was brought about by a John Borbot and his sister, Evelyn, when they dismantled a nightclub in Dollarville in 1939 and reconstructed it at Christmas (the town), and called it the Knotty Klub. It was officially the first business in town and was followed by motels, gift shops, two grocery stores, a restaurant, and another bar.

For tourists, the town of Christmas became another destination point just down the road from Pictured Rocks. The Christmas (the holiday) name and theme has drawn people to it time and time again, to enjoy the ambiance the little town offered that reminded visitors that every day could be Christmas (the holiday). The idea has worked well throughout the past eighty years. In July 1966, Christmas (the town) received a postal substation, which officially designated it as a town. When the substation opened on July 8, there was a rush from stamp collectors from all over the world to get first-day cancellations on stamps from Christmas. That November, when the postal service issued its five-cent Christmas (the holiday) stamp, there was a big ceremony with local politicians attending, and an official dedication of the post office was held. The Christmas (the holiday) stamp with the Christmas (the town) cancellation was quite a collector's item.

When it was determined that Christmas would actually become a town, a controversy arose over who had actually named the area. Was it actually Julius Thorson, or was it George Mitchell, the man who was also behind Christmas Industries? George Mitchell was involved with Thorson in the ill-fated project. His actual role in the business has been obscured by time, but it has been determined that he was either the money behind the project or the man Thorson hired to run it. Different accounts state different opinions.

When the Christmas stamp was issued with the first Christmas cancellation, Mitchell, who was a stamp collector and dealer in Homestead, Florida, perpetuated the rumor by claiming, in Florida, that he had named the town "Christmas." He told his story to one of the Florida newspapers and word of his claims filtered north. It started a debate between local Alger county individuals and historians over who actually registered the name to the Christmas plat.

Finally, in a letter sent by Mitchell, he conceded that the name had been registered by Thorson and the controversy died down. To this day, though, the first stamp issued in Christmas is a collector's item and the publicity Mitchell received and his dealership surely didn't hurt his sales in Florida.

Getting a letter or card cancelled in the town of Christmas at this time of year has become a big tradition, and every year, thousands of people receive mail containing one of these stamps. Even local businesses offer personalized letters from Santa with, of course, the now famous Christmas seal of authenticity.

The people who live in Christmas (the town) celebrate the holiday Christmas, just like anyone else, with their family and friends, but the holiday is never far from their thoughts. It is a tradition that is capitalized on all year, and that isn't at all bad. Many people try to keep the spirit of Christmas alive all year long and the people of Christmas certainly have a head start.

With their statues, businesses, street names (like Santa Claus Lane etc.), and their sense of fun, it's always Christmas in Christmas and it's right here in the U.P. It is a small charismatic little place that, even if you don't stop, leaves you with a smile and some thoughts about this special holiday, no matter what time of year you visit or pass through there. In Christmas the town, it's Christmas the holiday, all year long.

14 November Victims: The Trial and Tragedy of The Steamer *Myron*

Fig. 14-1: The SS Myron as it appeared in port before the tragic wreck. Here it is loaded with lumber on the deck (Wikipedia).

There have been many tragedies across the Great Lakes over the years, especially in the month of November, but few have as strange and grim a story as that of the *Myron*. One reason for this is, there were witnesses and a survivor. Few accounts are as complete and controversial as this one. From a November gale, to a ship in distress, a rescue effort that failed and a maritime hearing for "Criminal Behavior" on the parts of would-be rescuers, this stands in the annals of shipwreck history as one the most unusual.

On November 22, 1919, the small steamer *Myron* set out from Munising, Michigan on its way to Buffalo, NY with a load of lumber. In tow was a schooner barge named the *Miztec*. Many of the old

Fig. 14-2: SchoonerMiztec with masts, before conversion to a barge (Wikipedia)

schooners had been refitted as barges and towing them behind a lead ship was common practice. These "barges" required a small crew and this one was no exception, there being 7 men aboard while 17 crewed the *Myron*. The Captain of the *Myron* was a seasoned veteran named Walter R. Neal.

About two hours out, a nasty November gale blew up. The waves built and began to pound on the two ships mercilessly. Captain Neal steamed his ship eastward as hard as he could, battling the ever-rising surf. The beating slowly caused the seams in the hull to begin separating and she started taking on water. She became heavier and unable to crest the waves. Then it started to snow.

The temperature began to fall. It was quickly becoming the deadliest of situations. Ice began to build up on both ships, changing their center of gravity, making them unstable.

Not far away was a ship named the *Adriatic*. Captain McRae had been watching the smaller ships and realized they were in obvious trouble. He brought his 420 foot ship around, steamed in close and attempted to shield the *Myron* and *Miztec*. He paced them, trying to keep them in the lee of the wind and surf.

At Vermillion Point, Captain Neal made a decision. If they were ever going to reach Whitefish Point, they would have to do it without the Miztec. This was a good, sound decision. Now the Miztec would be free to weather the storm on its own without being tethered to the Myron. Captain Neal ordered the tow rope released and continued on without her. The Miztec dropped anchor, put its bow to the waves and miraculously survived the storm.

The *Myron* pushed on with the Adriatic still shadowing it. A lookout at the Vermillion Life Saving Station spotted the two ships and sounded the alarm. The life saving crew scrambled and launched their motor-powered surfboats into the teeth of the gale. It was what they did. None of them believed the *Myron* would ever make Whitefish Point. None of them believed the crew could survive Lake Superior's wrath. They chased the *Myron* in a desperate race to save the crew's lives. The Coast Guardsmen didn't make it in time.

About a mile and a half from Whitefish Point, water reached the Myron's boilers and she lost all power. The powerless, swamped ship dropped into a deep trough of water, releasing the cargo of lumber into the water. Everyone knew this was the end for the Myron. The crew scrambled to the lifeboats and were successful in releasing and launching them just before the doomed ship went under. Captain Neal stayed on board.

Floating around the lifeboats was an immense field of wreckage from the steamer and its cargo. The crewmen worked to get away from it but they were completely surrounded. The lifeboats were trapped within. Darkness was fast closing in and so was hypothermia.

Captain McRae moved the *Adriatic* toward the lifeboats. The ship rose and fell in the troughs of the Lake Superior waves. Beneath his feet, the Captain felt the *Adriatic* hit bottom. Then she hit again. McRae turned the ship about and refused to make another attempt for fear his ship would run aground.

In the distance, another ship had been watching the unfolding disaster. The *H.P. McIntosh*, an even bigger ship than the *Adriatic*, saw the *Adriatic* fail and decided they might be able to make it. Through the rough seas it plowed and pushed its way through the wreckage. The *Myron*'s crew watched with hope as Captain Lawrence maneuvered his ship close enough to throw ropes out to the freezing crewmen. Cold and numb, they reached out for the lines. They couldn't hang on to them. Their limbs were too cold and the effort failed. Also fearing for his ship, Captain Lawrence withdrew and headed for open water.

The Vermillion Coast Guard Life Savers had now caught up with the *Myron* and attempted to reach the survivors. The floating mass of spars and lumber churning in the gale-driven surf kept them too far away. They could not complete a rescue either. The two lifeboats of half frozen men were left to their fate. They all died.

The bodies of the crew were found frozen in lifejackets. They were covered in ice and in horrible, grotesque shapes. The bodies recovered immediately were sent to the Soo and a funeral home where they had to thaw the bodies out by a fire. The next spring, eight of them were discovered frozen into shore ice at Salt Point north of Bay Mills. They were chipped out of the ice and buried at Mission Hill Cemetery in Bay Mills.

Two days after the *Myron* sank, near Parisienne Island, a survivor was discovered. The *H.C Franz* was sailing Whitefish Bay looking for bodies when they came across the *Myron*'s pilot house still floating. Clinging to it was Captain Neal. As the *Myron* sank the pilot house tore loose and Neal had been able to climb through one of the windows and had been floating ever since. Nearly frozen, but still alive, his hands had swelled so bad, two rings he was wearing were no longer visible on his fingers. He was rescued and brought back to the Soo.

When he recovered, he accused the Captains of the *Adriatic* and the *H.P. McIntosh* of criminal behavior over their failures to rescue his crew. A hearing was held by the Steamboat Inspection Service to look into the accusations.

In the hearing, Captain Neal testified about his own experience. "I was clinging to the roof of the pilot house when the *McIntosh* hailed me shortly after the *Myron* went down from under me. The McIntosh drew alongside me, not more than 16 feet away. Although it was dusk, the ship was so close that I had no difficulty in making out her name. I talked to the Captain and expected that he would put out a yawl and pick me up. He did not do so, nor attempt in any way to help me. 'I will have a boat sent for you,' the Captain of the *McIntosh* called. And he drew away. I have never seen him since, nor do I ever want to see him, by the great hokey pokey."

Captain Neal's accusations stuck and the Steamboat Inspection Service revoked the licenses of both captains for life for "failure to render aid and assistance." Many felt this penalty was too stiff because of the efforts that were made, but it appears there was never an appeal. Captain Neal would sail again.

In a strange coincidence, the *Miztec*, the schooner barge that survived the ordeal, sank two years later in nearly the same location as that of the *Myron*.

15 Peter White: The Founding of Marquette and the Story Surrounding It

Fig. 15-1: This is an old drawing of Marquette as it looked in 1851, very close to the time in Peter White's Narrative.

This is a firsthand account by the Honorable Peter White about his arrival in Marquette and the founding of the city in his own words. Peter White spoke of this in 1870, offering a glimpse into the years 1850-1853 on the Lake Superior frontier. His wry wit comes through in the narration, and the life and death stories contained within almost feel like "just another day in the life." This recounts the felling of the first trees for the city, the arrival of the earliest citizens, disease outbreak, mutiny, daring rescues, and brutal survival in the wilderness. This is a glimpse into the U.P. of the past that is unlike any other.

Peter White not only helped clear the land that would be Marquette, but was instrumental in getting the Soo Locks built, was a postmaster and served as a legislator and state senator. He worked on getting the first school district organized and established the first library. His legislation got a railroad built from the Sault to Marquette. Peter

White not only was a founding father of Marquette, but much of his work left lasting changes across the whole of the Upper Peninsula of Michigan. His credibility makes the account below priceless. Rarely do we get such a complete look into the origins of a city, and the struggle against the Lake Superior wilderness.

In the words of Peter White:

> It was from this island (Mackinac), twenty-one years ago this month, that the little (and I might say almost worthless) steamer *Tecumseh* took her departure for Sault Ste. Marie. It was a tempestuous April morning: the seas rolled mountain high and before she had accomplished many miles, a huge wave took off the yawl boat, swept through the steamer's gangways, washed overboard much of the freight from the decks, alarmed the passengers and brought Capt. Pratt to the conclusion that he had better turn his craft and run her for the haven of safety he had left only a few hours before. The steamer was not as fleet as the famous chief whose name she bore. He could probably have beaten her best speed on foot and through a thicket. Still, she did reach her starting point and after a delay of 24 hours for repairs, she again started on her trip. There were many more passengers on board than the boat had either eating or sleeping accommodations for, but it was not intended that she should be more than twelve hours in making the trip.
>
> On board was a party specially bound to settle and start the city of Marquette and to claim and undertake to develop all of the iron mountains that had been or should subsequently be discovered. The head and leader of this party was Robert J. Graveraet. At that time, he was a fit leader for any great enterprise that required the exercise of pluck, energy, and perseverance. He had an indomitable will, a commendable ambition and a splendid physical organization capable of enduring an untold amount of fatigue; a disposition firm, yet gentle and generous to a fault, a figure that, for grace, beauty, noble bearing and symmetrical proportions, I have never seen equaled. He had many virtues, but his end was sad indeed. Many a man without a tithe of the noble qualities he possessed holds a place in history as a great hero.
>
> The lively little steamer (lively with bedbugs), after thrashing around for several hours, finally got inside the Detour, and

Fig. 15-1: Peter White around 1860, about 10 years after he came to the Marquette area as a settler.

there met with solid ice, two to three feet thick, and there were no indications of a speedy thaw. The boat was run about half her length into the ice, when some of the passengers debarked and ran up it in all directions. Some essayed the cutting of a canal with saws and axes, but soon gave it up as a slow job. The next day we backed out and tried another passage, by way of the Bruce Mines, and thus succeeded in hammering our way through to the Sault in just ten days from the time we left Mackinac. In the meantime we had a bread riot, an insurrection, and once the boat sank to her deck, full of water. (Author's Note: To clarify this last bit, the ship was overloaded and had only planned food for a 12 hour trip, not 10 days.] Fed up with this the passengers decided to revolt but just as their ad hoc mutiny began, the ship began to sink.) She should have remained there, perhaps, forever, but for the aid of an old fellow we had named "Old Saleratus," and at whom we had poked all manner of fun. He proved to be a ship carpenter, and, after we had unloaded the boat and pumped her up, he found the leak, put in a new plank and we proceeded on our way.

We succeeded in crowding our large Mackinac barge up the rapids, or falls, at Sault Ste. Marie, and embarking ourselves and provisions, set sail on Lake Superior for the Carp River Iron Region. After eight days of rowing, towing, poling and sailing, we landed on the spot immediately in front of where Mr. George Craig's dwelling now stands. That was then called Indian Town, and was the landing place of the Jackson Company. We put up that night at the cedar house of Charley Bawgam (Kawbawgam). It is true his rooms were not many, but he gave us plenty to eat, clean and well cooked. I remember that he had fresh venison, wild ducks and geese, fresh fish, good bread and butter, coffee and tea, and splendid potatoes.

The next morning, we started for the much-talked-of iron hills; each one had a pack-strap and blanket, and was directed to exercise his own discretion in putting into a pack what he thought he could carry. I put up forty pounds and marched bravely up the hills with it for a distance of two miles, by which time I was about as good as used up. Graveraet came up, and, taking my pack on top of his, a much heavier one, marched on with both, as if mine was only the addition of a feather, while I trudged on behind, and had hard work to keep up. Graveraet seeing how fatigued I was, invited me to get on top of his load, saying he would carry me, too, and he could have done it, I believe; but I had too much pride to accept his offer.

When we arrived at the little brook which was by George Rublein's old brewery, we made some tea and lunched, after which I felt so much refreshed that I took my pack and carried it without much difficulty to what is now known as the Cleveland Mine, then known as Moody's location. On our way we had stopped for a few minutes at the Jackson Forge, where we met Mr. Everett (discoverer of the Marquette iron deposits), Charles Johnson, Alexander McKerchie, A.N. Barney, N.E. Eddy, Nahum Keyes, and some others. At the Cleveland we found Capt. Sam Moody and John H. Mann, who had spent the previous summer and winter there. I well remember how astonished I was the next morning when Capt. Moody asked me to go with him to dig some potatoes for breakfast. He took a hoe and an old tin pail, and we ascended a high hill, now known as the Marquette Iron Company's Mountain, and on the pinnacle found half an acre partially cleared and planted to potatoes. He opened but one or two hills when his pail was filled with large and perfectly sound potatoes—and then said, "I may as well pull a few parsnips and carrots for dinner, to save coming up again,"—and, sure enough, he had them there in abundance. This was in the month of May.

From this time till the 10th of July, we kept possession of all of the iron mountains then known west of the Jackson, employing all of our time fighting mosquitoes at night, and the black flies through the day; perhaps a small portion of it was given to demanding the iron hills of extraneous matter, preparing the way for the immense products that have since followed. On the 10th of July we came away from the mountains, bag and baggage, arriving at the lake shore, as we then termed it, before noon. Mr. Harlow had arrived with quite a number of mechanics, some goods, lots of money, and, what was better than all, we got a glimpse of some female faces. We were all much excited and buoyant with the hope of a bright and dazzling future before us.

At 1 o'clock of that day, we commenced clearing the site of the present city of Marquette, though we called it Worcester in honor of Mr. Harlow's native city. We began by chopping off the trees and brush, at the point of rocks near the blacksmith shop, just south of the shore end of the Cleveland Ore Docks. We cut the trees close to the ground, and then threw them bodily over the bank onto the lake shore; then, under the direction of Capt. Moody, we began the construction of a dock, which was to stand like the ancient pyramids, for future ages to wonder at and admire! We did this by carrying these whole trees into the water and piling them in tiers, crosswise, until the pile was even with the surface of the water. Then we wheeled sand and gravel upon it, and, by the end of the second day, we had completed a structure which we looked upon with no little pride. Its eastward or outward end was solid rock, and all inside of that was solid dirt, brush and leaves. We could not see why it should not stand as firm and as long as the adjacent beach itself! A vessel was expected in a few days, with a large lot of machinery and supplies, and we rejoiced in the fact that we had a dock upon which they could be landed.

On the third day, we continued to improve it by corduroying the surface, and by night of that day, it was, in our eyes, a thing of beauty to behold. Our chagrin may be imagined, when on our rising the next morning, we found that a gentle sea had come in during the night and wafted our dock to some unknown point. Not a trace of it remained; not even a poplar leaf was left to mark the spot. The sand of the beach was as clean and smooth as if it had never been disturbed by the hand of man. I wrote in the smooth sand with a stick, "This is the spot where Capt. Moody built his dock." The Captain trod upon the record, and said I would get my discharge at the end of the month, but he either forgot or forgave the affront. It was a long time before anyone had the hardihood to attempt the building of another dock.

The propellers would come to anchor sometimes as far as two miles from the shore, and the freight and passengers had to be landed in small boats. Our large boilers, when they arrived, were plugged, thrown overboard and floated ashore, and the other machinery was landed with our Mackinac boat or a scow which we had constructed. Cattle and horses were always pitched overboard and made to swim ashore.

Under the lead of James Kelly, the boss carpenter, who was from Boston, we improved our time, after 6 o'clock each evening, in erecting a log house for sleeping quarters for our particular party. When finished, we called it the Revere House, after the hotel of that name in Boston. This building stood on its original site as late as 1860.

About this time, we realized the necessity of procuring hay for our stock. A man called Jim Presque Isle informed Capt. Moody that he knew of a large meadow a short distance above Presque Isle, covered with superb blue-joint grass; the only trouble was that it was flooded with water too deep to admit of mowing, but he thought we could, with shovels, in a few hours, cut a drain out to the lake which would carry the water off. So off we started in our boat, armed with shovels, axes, scythes, rakes and pitchforks. Capt Moody nervously staked out the ground for the canal, and we dug each way from the center for four or five hours and at last opened both ends simultaneously, when, to our consternation, the waters of the lake rushed in and raised that of the meadow three or four inches! We were not more than five minutes embarking all of our tools and getting off. We tried to keep still about the matter, but it leaked out some way, and was the source of a great deal of sport.

We continued clearing up the land south of Superior Street, preparing the ground for a forge, machine shop, sawmill and coal house. Some time in August, the schooner Fur Trader arrived, bringing a large number of Germans, some Irish and a few French. Among this party were August Machts, George Rublein, Francis Dolf, and Patrick, James and Michael Atfield. All these have resided here continuously up to the present time, have been and are good citizens, and have become men of property. Gravaraet and Clark had been to Milwaukee and hired and shipped them on a vessel. It was the Cholera year; Clark died at the Sault on his way back; several others had died on the vessel, and many were landed very sick. We were all frightened; but the Indians, who lived here to the number of about one hundred, had everything embarked in their boats and canoes within sixty minutes, and started over the waters to escape a disease to them more fearful than the small pox.

Now the medical talent of Dr. Rogers was called into requisition. He laid aside the hoe and ax he had learned to handle so dexterously and took up the practice of his profession. It was found, on examination, that there were no real cases of cholera, but many of the newcomers had the typhoid or ship fever, and that it was contagious was soon evident, for the doctor, and perhaps a dozen of our young men who had never known sickness before were soon stricken down with it. Each one of my companions had, in succession, had taken the position of nurse in the hospital (a rude building called a hospital had been erected), and had in regular order been taken down with the malignant fever.

It was my turn next; I looked upon it as a new promotion, abandoned my oxen, glad of a change, having no fear that I would catch the fever, and I did not. About the time I went in, Dr. Rogers was very low, indeed, unable to lisp a word, and to this fact I attribute the recovery of himself and associates; for, as I knew nothing of medicines, I discarded them altogether, and, by advice of Mr. Harding, Mr. Emmons and Mrs. Wheelock, I commenced rubbing and bathing them, and Mrs. Wheelock furnishing suitable food, the result was that in two weeks they were all convalescent. Dr. Rogers often said afterward, "If I could have told the fool what medicine to give, he would have killed us all."

At this time the first steam boiler ever set up in this county was ready to be filled with water, and it must be done the first time by hand. It was a locomotive boiler, and was afterward put into the side-wheel steamer *Fogy*, which plied between Marquette and Chocolay so many years. A dollar and a half was offered for the job, and I took it; working three days and a night or two, I succeeded in filling it. Steam was got up and I then was installed as engineer and fireman.

That summer there were but few boats of any kind on the lake. The propeller Independence was generally broken down, and the little propeller Napoleon only came three or four times during the season. The reliable mail, freight and passenger craft was the Fur Trader, commanded by the veteran Capt. Ripley, from whom the picturesque rock in Marquette Bay took its name. The *Fur Trader* was a small sail vessel, and usually made a trip in three or four weeks; but it was toward the last of October, and neither she nor any other craft had put in an appearance for nine or ten weeks. The stock of provisions was quite low; the butter and luxuries of all kinds were wholly exhausted; only a few barrels of pork and flour remained, and the danger of being put on very short rations was imminent.

Then Mr. Harding discovered, or pretended to discover, a conspiracy among the Germans to seize the warehouse and confiscate what provisions were left. He volunteered to command a guard to watch the warehouse day and night. The provisions were doled out sparingly, the Germans becoming very much dissatisfied, and, a short time after (in November), they "struck," and a large number of them started out of the country, intending to follow the lake shore to Grand Island, and go from there overland to Little Bay de Noquette. (Little Bay de Noc) Only a few reached Grand Island; the weaker ones, foot-sore, weary and hungry, lagged at different points along the beach, and probably many of them would have perished but for the return of those of the party who had reached Grand Island, and there learned that a propeller, loaded with provisions had arrived here the next day after they left. So they returned, and the cheering news revived the drooping spirits of their comrades, as they came up to them here and there along the beach, and they finally all got back, wiser, and better men. None of the Germans named as still residing here went off with the party.

On the 27th of November, our boat was started for Sault Ste. Marie in charge of James Hilliard (sometimes called Jim Presque Isle). John H. Mann, Mr. Emmons and a German boy named Kellogg, accompanied him. They were all drowned, the boat being afterward found with two bodies in it, while the body of Mr. Emmons was not recovered till the following spring.

As I have told two stories that militate against Capt. Moody's skill as an engineer, it is only fair that I should relate one which redounds to his credit as a navigator. We had by some means been apprised of the fact that the schooners Swallow and Siskiwit, which had been loaded with grain and supplies for us at Sault Ste. Marie, had run by and laid up for the winter at L'Anse. The grain was absolutely necessary to keep the horses from starving. Capt. Moody promptly started for L'Anse, accompanied by James Broadbent, an old salt water sailor.

On their arrival there, they found both the vessels stripped and laid up, and, what was worse, frozen in the ice. But Moody had pluck enough to undertake any task, no matter how difficult or dangerous. He and his man went to work at once to refit one of the vessels—the *Siskiwit*—on the principle that might makes right. They paid no attention whatever to the urgent protests of her owner, Capt. James Bendry. They filled her with corn and oats from the Swallow, and employed a large number of Indians to cut a passage between two and three miles long, through the ice, so as to float the vessel out into the open water. They got her out on Christmas Eve, and arrived here on Christmas Day, the sails frozen stiff and immovable, and the ice a foot thick on her deck. They had not seen land from the time they left L'Anse until they reached Marquette Bay, a heavy northwest gale and snowstorm prevailing all the time. The vessel was unloaded and run into the Chocolate River, where she lay until spring, when, in coming out, she ran on the beach and went to pieces.

During that winter we had three or four mails only. Mr. Harlow was the first postmaster and hired the Indian, Jimmers, to go to L'Anse after the mail at a cost of $10 per trip. I believe the cost was made up by subscription.

The Jackson Company had about suspended operations; their credit was at a low ebb; their agent had left in the fall, and was succeeded by "Czar" Jones, the President, but nearly all work was stopped, and the men talked seriously of hanging and quartering Mr. Jones, who soon after left the country. In the spring the Jackson Company "bust" all up, and all work at their mine and forge was suspended. By this time, the Marquette Iron Company's forge was nearly completed and ready for making blooms. Many dwellings, shops, etc., had been erected, together with a small dock at which steamers could land. This dock still forms the shore end of the Cleveland Company's merchandise pier.

In the fall of 1850, B.F. Eaton, and his brother, Watt Eaton, arrived from Columbus, Ohio. They had leased the old Jackson

Forge and Mine, and brought with them an immense number of men and horses, and a large quantity of supplies. They commenced operations with a grand flourish of trumpets and high sounding words that bid fair to eclipse and crush everybody else out of existence in short order. They burst all to pieces within a year, and never paid their men a dollar in money; those who took goods for pay were wise. Ben Eaton was so disgusted with the country that he finally left the United States and went to Australia and, as far as I know, has never returned.

In the summer of 1851, we had pretty hard times generally, no money, and not much of anything else. I think it was in September of that year the county was organized. I was absent up the lake shore, fishing at the time, and, on my return, was informed that I had been elected County Clerk and Register of Deeds. I told my informant (Amos Parish) that I was not of age; to which he replied that the impression generally prevailed that I was over thirty, that no one would say anything if I did not, and that it was very desirable to have someone hold those offices who could write. I was flattered and consented. Up to this time, we had been attached to Houghton County, the county seat being at Eagle River.

On one occasion, I was sent, in the dead of winter, on foot and alone, up to Eagle River to get the County Clerk's certificate to a lot of legal documents. I went to L'Anse, thence across the ice to Portage Entry, up the river, over Portage Lake, and across the Portage to Eagle River. I called on Mr. Kelsey, the County Clerk, and attended to the business I had in hand. He inquired, "When do you return?" "Tomorrow." "Oh no," said he; "we never allow a winter visitor to depart under two weeks, and, as you are the first man who has ever come from Marquette or Carp River up here by land, we must give you a good time."

Mr. S.W. Hill and Henry Parke came in, and between the three they agreed that I should have a big party the next night. The thought occurred to me whether I had not better cut and run for home, but I concluded if I should, and they caught me, it would go hard with me; so, I resolved to stay, and, if necessary, run the gauntlet, or fight for my liberty if cornered.

The next day, Dr. L.W. Clarke, John Senter, George Senter, William Morrison, William Webb, Joe Thatcher and others called, paid their respects and tendered various civilities. I watched them all closely, but could not discover that my suspicions of conspiracy against me were well founded. The gay party came off the next evening, and all my fears were dispelled. I was invited the next night to a party at Eagle River, and, when I argued that my apparel was not suited for parties, I was forcibly taken into Senter's store, and there compelled to put on an elegant suit of clothes; and for the next eight or ten days I was put through such a round of pleasures and hospitable attentions never before nor since witnessed by me. I could not have been more civilly feasted and toasted had I been the President. Such was the hospitality of the early settlers of the copper region.

At last, when I was about to leave, I was offered silver specimens, agates, or anything else they had. My wants were, however, few and simple, and I said, "Give me two cans of those elegant cove oysters to take back to my Carp River friends, and I will be delighted." I worked my way back as far as Portage Entry, and found the ice in L'Anse Bay all broken up. Mr. Ransom Shelden then lived at the Entry, buying fish and furs from the Indians. At that day, copper mining on Portage Lake had not been dreamt of. After my arrival at the Entry, I was laid up for three days with the "Le mal de Racket" or snowshoe sickness. As soon as I could travel, I set out through the woods for the Catholic Mission. I knew nothing of the route except to keep in sight of the bay, and that I soon found was impracticable, owing to the impenetrable nature of the underbrush; so I struck back for better walking.

The distance I had to go to reach the mission was sixteen miles, and it seemed to me I had travelled thirty. I had no dinner. It was very cold—twenty-two degrees below zero—the 18th of January; night was close at hand. I crossed a little valley, and, as I mounted the hill, I looked back of me and caught the only glance of the sun I had that day. I knew that to reach the mission I ought to be going toward the setting sun! I turned my course in that direction, and, in a short time, came across a single snowshoe track, and was much pleased to think I was getting where some one else had so recently been. Before long I crossed another track similar to the first, and soon a third. A little closer examination convinced me that they were all my own tracks, and that for hours I had been travelling on a circle, only enlarging it a little each time.

It was now rapidly growing dark. Fortunately I had matches, but I had no ax, nor any provisions, except the two cans of cove oysters. I succeeded in starting a fire at the foot of a dead cedar that leaned over into the forks of a hemlock, and, as fast as it would burn to a coal, it would slide down a little, and thus my fire was replenished all night. I was too much excited to be either tired or hungry that night. I slept some in an upright or sitting posture, before the fire; the snow was about five feet deep, and I had shaped an indentation of my own figure, like a chair, into the snow, and lined it with balsam boughs, so that it was quite comfortable.

In the morning, after breaking all the blades of my Congress knife in opening one of the cans of "elegant cove oysters," I boiled them in the can and tried to eat them; but it was hard work; they wouldn't stay down. Through the kindness of the good Bishop Baraga, who knew that I was either hurt or lost (he had left the entry after I did), an Indian was sent out, and found me about 3 o'clock, and before dark I was safely housed at the mission. After many more hardships, I succeeded in reaching home.

I have merely touched upon some of the incidents of the first two or three years of the history of Marquette and the iron region. A few houses, a stumpy road winding along the lake shore; a forge which burnt up after impoverishing its first owners; a trail westward, just passable for wagons, leading to another forge (still more unfortunate in that it did not burn up), and to the undeveloped iron hills beyond; a few hundred people uncertain of the future – these were all there was of Marquette in 1851-52.

Little did we think that the region we came to settle would, in so short a time, be known and felt everywhere; that the mineral products would be borne by hundreds of vessels to the ports of all the Great Lakes. The Sault Canal was then a project the consummation of which was devoutly wished, but not realized; and the boldest of us had not dreamed of a railroad from our little hamlet to the iron hills. We were building better than we know. We had fallen into the march of the century, not knowing whither it would lead us. We were like the fishermen of the Arabian Nights, who ignorantly opened a small sealed casket which they had drawn out of the sea in their nets. It held an imprisoned Genii, who emerged at first like a little vapor, which while they wondered, spread and ascended, until it towered up like a vast column toward heaven.

The forge was completed and made the first bloom in just one year from the day Mr. Harlow landed with his men. He started with four fires, using ores from what are now the Cleveland and Lake Superior Mines. It continued in operation, rather irregularly, until 1853, when the Marquette Company was merged into the Cleveland, under the auspices of which latter company the works were operated, until destroyed by fire in the winter of 1853.

Peter White Esq.—1870

16 The Strange Case of Reimund Holzhey

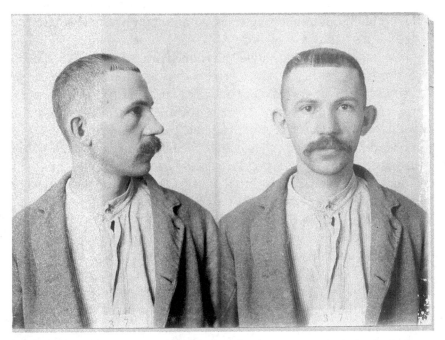

Fig. 16-1: Mugshot of Reimund Holzhey, also known as "Black Bart" the last stage coach robber of the midwest.

In 1889, a stagecoach on the way to Lake Gogebic was robbed. A man calling himself "Black Bart" stood in front of the stage with a shotgun and a pair of pistols. He ordered the passengers out of the coach and proceeded to divest them of their belongings. One of the passengers was having none of it and pulled a gun and fired. "Black Bart" fired back. In the ensuing chaos, the man who had drawn the gun was wounded and another passenger had taken a shot to the gut. The robber was unscathed. He rode away after relieving everyone of their valuables. A couple of days later, one of the passengers died, making "Black Bart" a murderer.

This "Black Bart" was not the same man as the famous stagecoach robber of the western states. He was actually named Reimund Holzhey (sometimes spelled Holshay), a German immigrant who took up a life of crime after coming to the U.S. He became enamored with dime novels and found the stories fascinating. At one point over 100 issues of different "heroes" of the west were found. Novels about the exploits of outlaws like Billy the Kid, Jesse James, and Black Bart fired his imagination and grew to hero worship. So much so that he adopted the name "Black Bart" and began living the life of an outlaw.

He spent some time in northern Wisconsin where he began a life as a thief robbing trains and stagelines. At one point he even broke into a judge's house and robbed him. A Wisconsin newspaper, the *Wood County Reporter*, wrote that he had robbed three stages, a Milwaukee and Northern passenger train, a general store at Bonduel, and a man in a carriage. Life was good for the thief, he managed to elude every posse that went after him and there was a $500 reward for his capture. It was then that he wandered into Gogebic County.

Everything changed on August 26th, 1889. A stageline ran from the south end of Lake Gogebic to Marinesco, Wisconsin. The road can still be found as Stagecoach Road to this day. (There is a historical plaque where the robbery occurred.) As the coach came down the road a man stepped out with two guns pointed at the coach. "Donate. I'm collecting," he said. There were four passengers in the coach. One of the passengers, (insert name), pulled a revolver saying "Here's mine," and fired a round at Holzhey. It missed completely. Holzhey instantly fired back emptying his guns, and the passenger fired off a couple of more rounds. In all the confusion one of the passengers was hit in the jaw and another passenger, Adolph Fleischbein in the thigh, the bullet travelling into his abdomen. It is unsure whose bullets hit whom. The guns going off caused the horses on the stagecoach to bolt and Fleischbein fell out of the coach onto the ground. Holzhey walked up and stood over him. He pointed a gun at Fleischbein's face and threatened to kill him. Truly afraid, he pleaded for his life invoking his wife and daughter. Holzhey agreed to spare his life, then took his wallet and jewelry and left Fleischbein lying in the road. It was more than two hours before help came.

Fleischbein lived long enough to tell his story, but died of his wounds a couple of days after the robbery. Holzhey was now a murderer and he was only twenty-two years old.

An intense manhunt began. They tracked Holzhey for six miles until they hit a stream and then they lost his trail. The next day they added bloodhounds and an Ojibwa tracker to the search, but again they came up empty. A drawing of Holzhey was published in the papers across the region. Deputies were posted along roads and at train stations throughout Gogebic County. A description of "Black Bart" went out, because his real name was as yet unknown. His description ran like this: "small in stature, dark, curling mustache, of medium height, slight build, and dressed in light clothes." A new reward was offered of $1000, mostly put up by the Milwaukee and Northern Railroad.

Holzhey had lit out for parts unknown hoping to get lost in the depths of the Upper Peninsula. He headed east to Republic, Michigan in Marquette County. This next part gets a little murky. There are several versions of the specifics, but the bottom line is that three or four days later, Holzhey turned up in Republic seemingly sure of himself in his anonymity. He went to hotel in Republic and registered as Henry Plant. The hotel clerk recognized him and called the local sheriff named Glode. They waited until morning and when Reimund walked out of the hotel, the sheriff and a couple of deputies grabbed him. There was a struggle and Holzhey went for his gun. The sheriff was too quick and grabbed it away from him while one of Glode's deputies popped Holzhey on the head. He had on him another revolver and a 12 inch bladed knife. When they searched him they found Fleischbien's wallet and personal effects in his pockets.

At the jail, Holzhey admitted to the robbery and all the others he had committed in Wisconsin. He complimented Glode on the job he had done and they went and had their pictures taken.

Holshey was shipped back to Bessemer to be housed in the Gogebic County Jail to await trial. It wasn't for long. On Sept. 27th Holzhey escaped, taking with him several other prisoners. The *Evening News of Detroit* described it like this, "Holzhay Escapes! The Michigan Bandit Again at Large. He Gets Out of Gogebic County Jail. Several Other Prisoners Escape With Him."

See the front cover of this book: "Reimund Holzey after his arrest in Republic, MI. Standing next to him is Sheriff Glode on the right and his Deputy."

Fig. 16-2: This was taken of Holzhey around the time of his trial in Bessemer. Taking his picture with all those weapons, it's no wonder he escaped.

The account goes on:

> "Reimund Holzhay, the train robber, stage robber, murderer, burglar, and general bandit who was captured a few days ago at Republic, Mich., has just escaped from the county jail here, along with several other prisoners. A general hue and cry has been raised, and the sheriff is calling upon every man he can reach in the city and country to take the trail of the desperate fugitive. If he is not overhauled at once, bloodhounds, which have been telegraphed for, will be put upon his trail, and should he make any resistance when overtaken it is altogether likely he may be killed on the spot. The most intense excitement prevails and the people are responding unanimously to Sheriff Foley's request to turn out. The attention of the pursuers will be devoted to Holzhay alone, unless he remains with the other escapees, and it will indeed be a miracle if he escapes capture. Telegrams are now being sent in every direction so as to anticipate the villain at all points of egress from this region."

It wasn't long and he was recaptured alive. Reimund was displaying such wild behavior that it caused many to question his sanity.

He was put on trial where he explained that his actions were due to an accident he had had early in his life when he'd spent some time out west. He claimed that a horse had fallen on him and had lain unconscious for a while. Holzhey said that he had been in good health before the accident, but afterward he felt bad from then on. Unable to describe how it felt, he claimed that it affected his entire system and particularly his head. He said he felt strange and many incidents that occurred during them were a blank. Holzhey even claimed to have visited different doctors over it.

A newspaper account from the *New York Tribune*, Nov. 15, 1889, describes it like this:

> "The spells came on him sometimes unexpectedly and he always had to look out for himself. At times he feels an irresistible impulse to do something bad or desperate. He has had several of these spells since his capture, and probably had a dozen or more since he was injured. Holzhey says that he remembered the day he was arrested and who arrested him. He could not tell why he held up the stage. He held it up and that was all he knew about it.

"In regard to holding up of the Wisconsin, Central and Milwaukee and Northern trains, Holzhey said he felt the spell about the same as at the time of the Gogebic stage robbery, and did not remember any of the incident connected with the affair. He stated that in all of these instances, where shooting was begun, it appeared to clear his brain and brought him to a realization of what he was doing, and he took to the woods afterward to avoid being captured. He said that he did not remember who was in the Gogebic Stage, did not remember seeing either Fleischbein or the driver, and failed to identify the watch and pocketbook said to have belonged to Fleischbein. He claimed that he had never seen Fleischbein's name on the pocketbook until his attention was directed to it."

When Holzhey was asked why he carried the guns when he was aware that he had fits, he replied, "I carried the revolvers to protect myself from wild animals in the woods, and did not like to leave them anywhere, as I might not be able to find them again." Holzhey himself was the only witness for the defense at his trial. He testified for two hours and was then returned to his cell. The jury retired to contemplate the case, but returned quickly. Holzhey was found guilty thanks to his confession and sentenced to life.

This bought him a trip to the Marquette Correctional Facility. There were rumors of a lynch mob waiting for him in Marquette, but one failed to materialize when he was taken off the train. Holzey didn't adjust well to prison life. Here he began to display some extreme behavior, violent outbursts, migraine headaches and even seizures.

Holzhey went off on the evening of March 6, 1890. He was getting out of there. One of the keepers, Palliser, came down to his cell and told him to come out. When he opened the door, Holzhey was too quick for him and grabbed him from behind and got a knife to the keeper's throat. He guided his hostage to a door and told the guard, "Kill me or I will kill this man." A deputy came up with a rifle intending to either shoot Holzhey or make him drop the knife. Holzhey was taunting the deputy by pushing Palliser away from him and then pulling him back. Suddenly Palliser used one of the pushes to break Holzhey's grip. He ran and Reimund gave pursuit but the keeper was faster. He got away, so Holzhey grabbed a prisoner who was close by and used him for a hostage.

The warden was on his way home, but was called back. He grabbed a gun and went to assess the situation. He found Holzhey with a knife to the throat of the prisoner. The standoff lasted long enough that Holzhey was getting tired. In the meantime the warden had been working his way along one of the upper galleries, hoping to get the drop on Holzhey, before he could spot him. Holzhey decided he and his hostage needed to sit down, which caused Holzhey to momentarily remove the knife from the man's throat. Warden Tompkins took his shot. It was perfect. He shot the knife from Holzhey's hand taking a thumb and a couple of fingers with it. All Holzhey could say was "Well, now you've done it."

He was placed into solitary and went on a hunger strike. He felt that losing part of his hand was punishment enough. A letter from Warden Tompkins to Governor Luce describes his condition. "He has taken but little food during the past four weeks, and not any the past ten days, except as the physician has forced it down his throat or injected it with a syringe. He has lost, I should think, fifty or sixty pounds of flesh since the trouble was had with him, and he refuses to answer questions or talk at all. His hand is entirely healed. I had hoped to get along without using a strap in this prison but I have just had one made. Unless something occurs to change my mind, I shall use it on Holzhey within the next few days."

There is no evidence on how Holzhey got past his food strike or whether he was forced out of it by the warden, but he returned into the general population of prisoners. He claimed to continue having spells and often stayed in his cell avoiding work duties. A new warden had arrived and decided to send Holzhey to Ionia Prison for the criminally insane.

It is here that doctors took Holzhey seriously. They discovered that a part of his skull had been fractured and was applying pressure to his brain. Supposedly it was something that happened to him as a child. It could be that the accident he claimed to have had with a horse during his trial may have caused it to affect him more severely. He was operated on and the pressure on his brain released. They then put in a silver plate to protect the damaged skull.

The operation changed Reimund Holzhey completely! He no longer acted out or was sullen. His violent rages were gone. He became a model prisoner. He was then sent back to Marquette.

Back in Marquette, Holzhey became active in his prison life. He developed a passion for photography and used his intellect to write for the prison newspaper. Restrictions were eased and he was allowed to do photos of the prison and became the official prison photographer. It

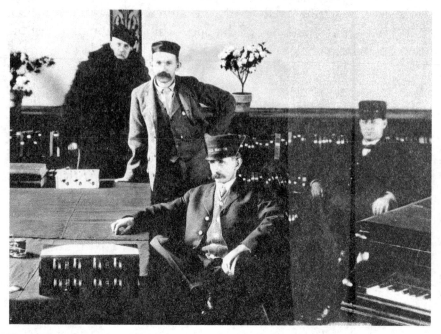

Fig. 16-3: Reimund Holzhey in prison after his operation. He began work on the prison newspaper. Holzhey is standing leaning on the table (courtesy Jack Deo - Superior View Studios.

is believed that he introduced the traditional front and side shot mug shot to the prison records. Most historical photos of the prison from this era are all shot by Holzhey. He was allowed to sell his photos through the prison gift store. He created clear glass paperweights that had photos on the bottom of various images of the prison.

Because of his turnaround, Holzhey was granted clemency in 1910 and was released in 1913. He had learned quite a few skills in prison that he hoped to put to use as he reentered the world. He wanted to stay around Marquette and often went into the surrounding woods to take photos. He then tried to open a photography studio in Marquette, but the community was against it, people being unable to put Holzhey's past behind them, and Reimund was forced to move on.

He wandered west, out to Yellowstone. He spent time photographing the region and then selling prints to tourists. His photography was his passion. Very little is known of him during this period until 1931.

His wanderings brought him to Captiva Island, one of the Sanibel Islands in Florida. He decided to stay there and built a cottage. He had considerable money, which he claimed he made on the stock market, but since it was only two years after the stock market crash, this seems highly unlikely. The entire country was facing the depression. Anyone having any amount of money was rare. Could Holzhey have had a stash of cash that he'd hidden from his train/stagecoach robbery days? It is an interesting possibility. When Holzhey was arrested after the Gogebic stage robbery, the only money found on him was Fleischbein's from the robbery itself. None of the money from the other robberies had ever been recovered. What happened to it?

Holzhey spent twenty-two years on the island. He wrote and photographed and was extremely well read. He used a sailing canoe to explore the island. One of the locals introduced him to a *National Geographic* writer who took a liking to him. They spent a lot of time together exploring the islands and he stayed with Holzhey long enough that Holzhey had a separate cottage built for the writer.

In 1953, at age 86, Holzhey shot himself on his porch at Captiva Island. One of the locals, a Clara Stran, who had been caring for him the few months before his death, indicates he was probably ill. She scattered his ashes at a bayou on the island called Blind Pass. In all the history of the Upper Peninsula, Holzhey's story is one of the strangest ever encountered. An outlaw, a thief, a murderer, a brawler, an intellectual, a writer, a photographer, a naturalist, all were the pieces that made up the complex character known today as the last stagecoach robber of the Midwest.

Bibliography

Alger County Historical Society, *Alger County—A Centennial History*, Bayshore Press, Munising, Michigan, 1986

Andreas, A. T., *History of the Upper Peninsula of Michigan*, Western Historical Company, Chicago, Illinois, 1883

Castle, Beatrice Hanscom, *The Grand Island Story*, John M. Longyear Research Library, Marquette, Michigan, 1987

Covert, William C. *Glory of the Pines: A Tale of the Ontonagon*. New York: Grosset & Dunlap, 1918.

Classen, Mikel B. *Au Sable Point Lighthouse: Beacon on Lake Superior's Shipwreck Coast*, 2014

Conway, Thor and Julie, *Spirits on Stone*, Heritage Discoveries Publications, San Luis Obispo, California 1975

Dickinson County, *Dickinson County Board of Commissioners*, Iron Mountain, Michigan, 1991

Dodge, Roy L., *Michigan Ghost Towns* Volume III Upper Peninsula, Glendon Publishing, Sterling Heights, Michigan, 1973

Elliott, Adele. *History of Fayette and Fairbanks Township*. Fayette, Mich.?: A. Elliott, 1900. Print.

Henry, Alexander, and James Bain. *Travels & Adventures in Canada and the Indian Territories between the Years 1760 and 1776.*, 2015. Internet resource.

Hill, Jack, *History of Iron County Michigan*, Norway Current, Norway, Michigan, 1976

Haley, William D, and James Philp. *Philps' Washington Described. a Complete View of the American Capital and the District of Columbia ... Edited by W.d.h.* New York, 1861 (account of Fr. Charlevoix).

Jamison, James K., *The Ontonagon Country*, Ontonagon Herald Company, Ontonagon, Michigan, 1948

Martin, John Bartlow, *Call It North Country*, Alfred Knopf, New York, 1944

McCommons, J. H.. *Camera Hunter: George Shiras III and the Birth of Wildlife Photography*. Albequerque, NM, University of New Mexico Press, 2021

Ontario Ministry of Natural Resources, *Agawa Indian Pictographs*, Ontario, Canada

Osborn, Chase S., *The Iron Hunter*, MacMIllan Company, New York, 1919

Peterson, Larry, *The Hiawatha Anthology*, Globe Printing, Ishpeming, Michigan, 2020

Pioneer Collections: Report of the Pioneer Society of the State of Michigan Together with Reports of County, Town, and District Pioneer Societies, Vol. 27. Lansing, Mich: Robert Smith, 1900. Print.

Reimann, Lewis C., *Hurley Still No Angel*, Northwoods Publishers, Ann Arbor, Michigan, 1954

Reimann, Lewis C., *Incredible Seney*, Avery Publishing, AuTrain Michigan, 1982

Schoolcraft, H. R., Eastman, S., & United States. *Historical and Statistical Information Respecting the History, Condition, And Prospects of the Indian Tribes of the United States: Collected and prepared under the direction of the Bureau of Indian Affairs per act of Congress of March 3rd, 1847.* Philadelphia: Lippincott, Grambo, 1851.

Stonehouse, Frederick, *Dangerous Coast Pictured Rocks Shipwrecks*, Avery Color Studios, AuTrain, Michigan, 1997

Stonehouse, Frederick, *Keweenaw Shipwrecks*, Avery Color Studios, AuTrain, Michigan 1988

Trout Lake Women's Club, *Tales and Trails of Tro-La-Oz-Ken*, Trout Lake Women's Club, Trout Lake, Michigan, 1976

Waring, Betty A., *Birch Michigan Gold N Memories*, Johnson Printing, Marquette, Michigan, 1991

Williams, Ralph D., *The Honorable Peter White*, Penton Publishing Company, Cleveland, Ohio, 1907

Newspapers & Periodicals

Daily News, Escanaba

Daily Northwestern, Oshkosh, WI

Chicago Tribune, Chicago, Illinois

Evening News, Detroit, Michigan

Evening News, Sault Ste. Marie, Michigan

Free Press, Detroit, Michigan

Daily Globe, Ironwood, Michigan

Daily Mining Gazette, Houghton, Michigan

Mining Journal, Marquette, Michigan

Munising News, Munising, Michigan

New York Times. New York, New York

Ontonagon Herald, Ontonagon, Michigan

Pioneer-Tribune, Manistique, Michigan

Schoolcraft County Pioneer, Manistique

Websites

https://lottamorgan.blogspot.com/2019/10/life-and-death-of-lotta-morgan.html

https://blogs.mtu.edu/archives/2019/10/25/flashback-friday-michigans-highwayman/

https://captivaislandhistoricalsociety.pastperfectonline.com/library/0FE EFE20-0D02-47C0-918E-923183164276

About the Author

Mikel B. Classen has been writing and photographing northern Michigan in newspapers and magazines for over thirty-five years, creating feature articles about the life and culture of Michigan's north country. A journalist, historian, photographer and author with a fascination of the world around him, he enjoys researching and writing about lost stories from the past. Currently he is managing editor of the *U.P. Reader* and is a member of the Board of Directors for the Upper Peninsula Publishers and Authors Association. In 2020, Mikel won the Historical Society of Michigan's, George Follo Award for Upper Peninsula History.

Classen makes his home in the oldest city in Michigan, historic Sault Ste. Marie. He is also a collector of out-of-print history books, and historical photographs and prints of Upper Michigan. At Northern Michigan University, he studied English, history, journalism and photography.

His book, *Au Sable Point Lighthouse, Beacon on Lake Superior's Shipwreck Coast*, was published in 2014 and his book, *Teddy Rooseveltand the Marquette Libel Trial*, was published in 2015, both by the History Press. He has a book of fiction called *Lake Superior Tales* published by Modern History Press, which won the 2020 U.P. Notable Book Award. His newest release is *Points North* a nonfiction travel book published in 2019 by Modern History Press. *Points North* has received the Historical Society of Michigan's, "Outstanding Michigan History Publication," along with the 2021 U.P. Notable Book Award.

To learn more about Mikel B. Classen and to see more of his work, go to his website at www.mikelclassen.com.

Index

Join us for epic adventures in the U.P. on land and lakes!
Pirates, thieves, shipwrecks, sexy women, lost gold, and adventures on the Lake Superior frontier await you! In this book, you'll sail on a ship full of gold, outwit deadly shapeshifters, battle frontier outlaws and even meet the mysterious agent that Andrew Jackson called "the meanest man" he ever knew. Packed with action, adventure, humor, and suspense, this book has something for every reader. Journey to the wilds of the Lake Superior shoreline through ten stories that span the 19th century through present day including "The Wreck of the Marie Jenny," "The Bigg Man," "Wolf Killer," and "Bullets Shine Silver in the Moonlight."

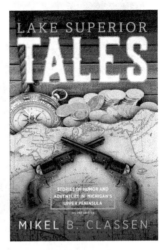

Mikel B. Classen is a longtime resident of Sault Sainte Marie in Michigan's Upper Peninsula. His intimacy of the region, the history and its culture gives this book a feel of authenticity that is rarely seen. As a writer, journalist, columnist, photographer, and editor with more than 30 years experience, his breadth of knowledge is unparalleled.

"It's clear that Mikel B. Classen knows and loves the Lake Superior area of Michigan and brings it to life in a delightful way. If you want frequent laughs, unusual characters who jump off the page, and the fruit of a highly creative mind, you've got to read this little book."
-- Bob Rich, author, *Looking Through Water*

"My favorite chapters were: Bullets Shine in the Moonlight; The Wreck of the Marie Jenny; Wolf Killers and Cave of Gold. It looks like you did your research and it was very well written. You kept me wanting to read more to find out what happens next."
-- Sharon Brunner, *U.P. Book Review*

Learn more at **www.MikelClassen.com**

paperback * hardcover * eBook * audiobook

ISBN 978-1-61599-404-5

Discover Your U.P. in *Points North* by Mikel Classen

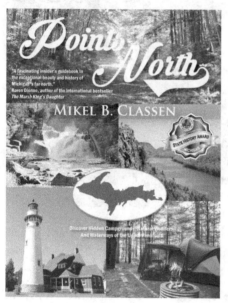

This book has been a labor of love that spans many years. The love is for Michigan's Upper Peninsula (U.P.), its places and people. I've spent many years exploring the wilderness of the U.P., and one thing has become apparent. No matter what part you find yourself in, fascinating sights are around every corner. There are parks, wilderness areas, and museums. There are ghost towns and places named after legends. There are trails to be walked and waterways to be paddled. In the U.P., life is meant to be lived to the fullest.

In this book, I've listed 40 destinations from every corner of the U.P. that have places of interest. Some reflect rich history, while others highlight natural wonders that abound across the peninsula. So many sights exist, in fact, that after a lifetime of exploration, I'm still discovering new and fascinating places that I've never seen or heard of. So, join in the adventures. The Upper Peninsula is an open book--the one that's in your hand.

"Without a doubt, Mikel B. Classen's book, *Points North*, needs to be in every library, gift shop and quality bookstore throughout the country--particularly those located in Michigan's Lower Peninsula. Not only does Classen bring alive the 'Hidden Campgrounds, Natural Wonders and Waterways of the Upper Peninsula' through his polished words, his masterful use of color photography make this book absolutely beautiful. *Points North* will long stand as a tremendous tribute to one of the most remarkable parts of our country."

--Michael Carrier, author *Murder on Sugar Island*

Learn more at www.PointsNorthBooks.com

paperback * hardcover * eBook * audiobook

ISBN 978-1-61599-490-8

The U.P. Reader:
Bringing Upper Michigan Literature to the World

Michigan's Upper Peninsula is blessed with a treasure trove of story-tellers, poets, and historians, all seeking to capture a sense of Yooper Life from 'settlers' days to the far-flung future. Now, U.P. Reader offers a rich collection of their voices that embraces the U.P.'s natural beauty and way of life, along with a few surprises.

The annually published volumes take readers on U.P. road and boat trips from the Keweenaw to the Straits of Mackinac. Every page is rich with descriptions of the characters and culture that make the Upper Peninsula worth living in and writing about. U.P. writers span genres from humor to history and from science fiction to poetry. This issue also includes imaginative fiction from the Dandelion Cottage Short Story Award winners, honoring the amazing young writers enrolled in the U.P.'s schools.

Whether you're an ex-pat, a visitor, or a native-born Yooper, you'll love U.P. Reader and want to share it with all your Yooper family and friends.

Available in paperback, hardcover, and eBook editions

To learn more: visit www.UPReader.org

From Modern History Press

CPSIA information can be obtained
at www.ICGtesting.com
Printed in the USA
JSHW042022220322
24099JS00002B/27

9 781615 996963